Sensory Perceptual Issues in Autism and Asperger Syndrome

of related interest

Asperger's Syndrome
A Guide for Parents and Professionals
Tony Attwood
ISBN 1 85302 577 1

Pretending to be Normal
Living with Asperger's Syndrome
Liane Holliday Willey
ISBN 1 85302 749 9

Freaks, Geeks and Asperger Syndrome
A User Guide to Adolescence
Luke Jackson
ISBN 1 84310 098 3

Can't Eat, Won't Eat
Dietary Difficulties and Autistic Spectrum Disorders
Brenda Legge
ISBN 1 85302 974 2

Build Your Own Life
A Self-Help Guide for Individuals with Asperger Syndrome
Wendy Lawson
ISBN 1 84310 114 9

Autism and Sensing – The Unlost Instinct
Donna Williams
ISBN 1 85302 612 3

Autism: An Inside-Out Approach
An Innovative Look at the Mechanics of 'Autism' and its Developmental 'Cousins'
Donna Williams
ISBN 1 85302 387 6

Sensory Perceptual Issues in Autism and Asperger Syndrome

Different Sensory Experiences – Different Perceptual Worlds

Olga Bogdashina

Forewords by Wendy Lawson and Theo Peeters

Jessica Kingsley Publishers
London and New York

First published in the United Kingdom in 2003
by Jessica Kingsley Publishers Ltd
116 Pentonville Road
London N1 9JB, England
and
29 West 35th Street, 10th fl.
New York, NY 10001–2299, USA

www.jkp.com

Library of Congress Cataloging in Publication Data
A CIP catalog record for this book is available from the Library of Congress

British Library Cataloguing in Publication Data
A CIP catalogue record for this book is available from the British Library

ISBN 1 84310 166 1

Printed and Bound in Great Britain by
Athenaeum Press, Gateshead, Tyne and Wear

I dedicate this book to my dearest children,
Alyosha and Olesya.
Being their mum is the best experience I've ever had.

Acknowledgements

My warmest thanks to

- all the autistic individuals who are willing to share their insights in order to help us understand this fascinating world of autism

- the parents who gave me their permission to use their children's drawings in this book

- the autistic children and teenagers I have had the privilege to work with for trying really hard to teach me to communicate with them

- my husband, Nigel Bath, for tolerating my 'absence' from his life during my 'writing hours'

- my beautiful children, Alyosha and Olesya, for their unconditional love, support and understanding.

Contents

8 Sensory Perceptual Profile   160

9 Recommendations: Rainbows and Umbrellas   170

Conclusion   181

Foreword

When I was asked to write a foreword to this book I felt excited and honoured. To read a book that puts forward 'our case' as autistic individuals is still a rarity. Although there is a wealth of books about 'autism' there is still so little that discusses our 'sensory issues' and their associations with cognitive style. This book is an important resource for both professionals and families relating to and living with autistic individuals. It is only in understanding that our knowledge can make sense of the world we all live in. Knowledge that is only 'academic' fails to move us along in any practical sense of the word and will fall short of imparting confidence to those who need it. This book aims to present a balanced view of how an autistic individual might be experiencing life, what his or her experience may be and how this experience may change over time. It is frank, to the point and paves the way to a fuller picture of 'personal autism'.

Many a time autistic individuals have been 'pushed' beyond their limits of sensory endurance. Often this is due to those relating to them not having understood how 'painful' it is to be overloaded by too much sound; visual stimulation; emotional or/and physical demand and environmental expectation. Those who read this book will now be able to access further the understanding necessary to prepare sensible and thoughtful programmes for any intended intervention or timetable. No longer will there exist any excuse for those who are involved in the daily activities of relating to an autistic individual to be ill prepared.

This book explores the outcomes of monotropic or single channelling: a constant state of being that is at the very core of what it means to be autistic; a state of being that non-autistic individuals can experience on occasion when they are focused to the max or perhaps taken up with an overwhelming thought or feeling, such as pain. The book considers the impact literality might have upon cognition. What if you couldn't separate an idiom from its literal translation? Might you feel terrified if someone said he had 'laughed his head off'? It demonstrates the extremes of emotion an autistic individual might travel through. Even today there is still literature that will tell you autistic individuals lack 'feeling'! This idea has been responsible for much of the abuse and misunderstanding that we have encountered as autistic people.

I still come across the thinking that allows an individual to say 'Oh she is doing that for attention' or 'He does understand what I'm saying, he is just too lazy to co-operate'. As autistic individuals we might not have the luxury of choosing to shift our attention. We might not even know what 'lazy' means. Such concepts are exploited more often by non-autistic individuals who know how to forward think, plot, plan and deliver! At times our very state as autistic individuals seems to threaten the neuro-typical (non-autistic) world because we show you up for who you are. Please don't be part of the 'us' and 'them' syndrome. Don't succumb to ignorance and typical thinking. Take the time to get to know 'autism'. Take the time to get to know us.

In a world that promotes inclusion and equal rights for all, what has happened to our 'right' to be autistic? What has happened to our 'right' to be heard? I think it has been buried under fear and ignorance for far too long. This book adds to the growing collection of works that is helping to address the ignorance behind the inappropriate dealings of others, i.e. those individuals who have not considered what it might mean to be an autistic individual. For those of you who have instinctively 'known us' this book will confirm your knowing and increase your confidence. To all who choose to relate to us using the knowledge outlined within the pages of this book, thank you. You are the individuals who will make a constructive difference to the quality of both of our lives.

Wendy Lawson
Counsellor, autism consultant and author

Foreword

My hearing is like having a hearing aid with the volume control stuck on 'super loud'. It is like an open microphone that picks up everything. I have two choices: turn the mike on and get deluged with sound, or shut it off. (Temple Grandin)

His mother says that he has to vomit whenever he smells cheese...And he says that his teacher stinks.

In my total horror of sounds, the sound of metal was an exception. I really like it. Unfortunately for my mother, the doorbell fell within this category and I spent my time obsessively ringing it. (Donna Williams)

It hurts if he touches buttons, zippers or anything in metal, but he may lay his hand upon a hot stove without feeling pain.

I was hypersensitive to the texture of food, and I had to touch everything with my fingers to see how it felt before I could put it in my mouth. I really hated it when food had things mixed with it, like noodles with vegetables or bread with fillings to make sandwiches. I could NEVER, NEVER put any of it into my mouth. I knew if I did I would get violently sick. (Sean Barron)

He says it hurts when he has a haircut, he refuses to take a shower, because it hurts, but he has a bath without problems.

Always the same problem: these kids have no education...

They really need to learn to be like everyone else...

Only give them to me for a week and I'll show them...

Thirty years ago, when I became more and more interested in autism, I started (as everyone, I think) reading the scientific literature and learned a lot, in a rational way.

But when I listened to the stories parents told I learned about aspects of autism that were more or less neglected by the official literature. Whereas the first type of information hit my brain, the second hit my heart. And I think that real understanding should include heart and brain together.

In recent years I have a similar feeling when I read books written by high functioning people with autism. Their understanding of autism is from within and they treat themes that are less well documented in the scientific literature. We can learn a lot from them (as they can learn a lot from us), about autism and sensory problems.

When, for example, I invited Gunilla Gerland ('A real person') a few years ago for conferences to the Opleidingscentrum Autisme (Centre for Training on Autism) in Antwerp and when I asked her about the themes she preferred to talk about, she answered that she certainly wanted to have a conference about sensory problems. Professionals in autism, she said, seem to focus too much on the triad.

> What professionals see as 'autistic' usually is – for natural reasons – what they can see, not what the autistic persons experience. Many people with Asperger syndrome/high functioning autism define their sensory processing problems as more disabling than the deficits in communication/social behaviour.

For our audience her conference on sensory problems really was an eye-opener.

In that period I also read *Autism: An Inside – Out Approach* by Donna Williams, who wrote that her problem in infancy was not so much that she did not understand the world, but that she could not stand it, because she was so often bombarded with an overload of sensory information.

Then I thought: if people with autism find this so important and if we understand these problems so little, then I have to study sensory aspects in autism more and write about it. And then came along this book written by

Olga Bogdashina (I do not have to write it anymore) and I like it so much that I'm a little bit jealous of not having written it myself.

Without mentioning the name 'Iceberg approach' she uses the same ethical approach towards autism as we do (I learned it at the TEACCH state program during my internship in North Carolina in 1979–1980). Basically it means: if you deal with 'challenging behaviours' in autism, do not focus too much on the behaviours themselves, they are just like the tip of the iceberg (the biggest part of the iceberg is invisible); do understand the underlying causes of the behaviours and try to develop an approach not based on symptoms but on prevention. Challenging behaviours are caused by problems of communication, social understanding, by different imagination, by sensory problems… Therefore try to understand autism 'from within'. It is easier said than done, because it requires an enormous effort of imagination: we need to learn to put ourselves in the brains of autistic people and then we will understand better through their eyes the obstacles in their attempts to survive among us.

This is also the basic orientation in Olga Bogdashina's book: she gives a lot of scientific information, but she also gives the word to the 'natives', the 'born experts' and all this with an attitude of enormous respect. For a better future cohabitation with people with autism we will indeed need to learn to look at life through 'the Asperger lens'.

> My teachers think they know more about autism than me because they have been on a course. But I have been autistic all my life!
> (Mathew Stanton)

'Trying to understand autism from within' is the first axis of our approach to understanding autism. In the first instance you need to try to share the mind of someone who is different.

I read Olga Bogdashina's manuscript when I was writing an article on 'Autism and the search for meaning'. I tried to explain how beyond behaviours that many people would call bizarre we may find a desperate search for meaning (e.g. beyond 'mindblindness', echolalia, echo-behaviour, detail thinking, repetitive and stereotyped behaviours, etc.). If you try to understand these 'odd behaviours' from within then you see that they may also have important functions for the people with autism themselves and that they are much less 'bizarre' than what people without the 'Asperger lens' would think. It makes me happy when I read Olga's analyses of so many sensory problems and how she shows (with the help of 'the native experts') how many behaviours have a protective function. Parents often say that the hardest thing to bear is that so many behaviours seem to have no meaning or function. Once they understand the cause of the behaviours they are less difficult to accept.

Donna Williams says about sensory issues of autism that they are like a private heaven under her own responsibility, but like a hell under the responsibility of others.

> When I was a small child my threshold for processing blah-blah was only a few seconds. When I was about ten or so, my threshold for processing blah-blah was about five to ten minutes.

It is in these circumstances of extreme stress that people with autism start humming, rocking, looking at turning objects, flapping hands and arms ('sensorisms', Olga calls them): 'self stimulatory behaviours', involuntary strategies the child has learned to cope with difficult situations (hypersensitivity) or lack of stimulation (hyposensitivity). Olga Bogdashina writes that it is unwise to stop these behaviours, however irritating and meaningless they seem. First we have to try to find out which functions these behaviours serve, so that we can replace them with experiences with the same function.

The second axis of our approach to understanding autism is 'the adaptation of the environment'.

We might also define it as 'trying to get people who live in chaos out of the chaos, so that they find some meaning and/or order. We have also called it 'pre-education' or 'creating circumstances where learning becomes possible'. As the quotes by Gunilla Gerland and Donna Williams (and so many other ones in this book) suggest: adapting to the sensory environment (and developing 'a sensory diet') is one of the essential elements of this 'pre-educational approach'. If people with autism have to live continuously in an environment that does not take into account their sensory sensitivity then they live in an atmosphere that makes me think of 'posttraumatic situations'. In such situations neuro-typical people also develop acute sensory problems. Information overload may lead to sensory and emotional hypersensibility and therefore to a situation of chronic stress '…it was not so much that I did not understand the world, I could not stand it…'. People who are not protected enough and who permanently have to fear that their central nervous system might crash are not in a position to learn difficult things and to face extra challenges.

I have selected a few fragments from *Autism: An Inside – Out Approach* when Donna Williams talks about an ideal educational environment:

> My ideal educational environment would be one where the room had verylittle echo or reflective light, where the lighting was soft and glowingwith upward projecting rather then downward project-ing lighting… It would be an environment where the educator's volume was soft, so that youhad to choose to tune in rather than being bombarded…
>
> It would be an environment that took account of mono and sensory hypersensitivity and information overload and didn't assume that the educator's perceptual, sensory, cognitive, emotional or social reality was the only one…
>
> There are many things that people with autism often seek to avoid: external control, disorder, chaos, noise, bright light, touch, in-volvement, being affected emotionally, being looked at or made to look. Unfortunately most educational environments are all about the very things that are the strongest sources of aversion.

There's still a lot of work ahead, don't you think?

Though this book is not the first to be published on sensory issues, I consider Olga Bogdashina a pioneer. With a monk's patience she has puzzled together so many testimonies of high functioning people with autism, she gives so many deep insights… Some people may say that some of the information may not be scientifically validated yet, but do you blame Icarus for flying too high? And isn't it extremely important that someone brings together all of this information and intuition to be researched later on? If the need of this type for information is so urgent, then there is no time to lose, no time to wait until every little detail has been scientifically proven.

One does not blame a blind child for not being able to name colours. And yet, youngsters with autism continue to be blamed despite their distorted, slower, faster perceptions… Many professionals, despite the evidence, continue to believe that many of these problems are of psychological, not of physiological origin. An educational approach, supplemented with sensory 'treatment', is not a question of how many hours, but of 'which perceptual world' we inhabit.

> Learning how the senses of each individual with autism function is a crucial key towards understanding this person. (O'Neill)

I agree completely with Olga Bogdashina when she says at the end:

> Stop trying to change them into 'normals'. Help them to cope with their problems and how to survive within the community.

Theo Peeters
Director of Centre for Training on Autism, Belgium

Introduction to the Problem

Since the first identification of autism in 1943 (Kanner), a lot of research has been carried out to study this condition from different perspectives. What has not been taken into account by the experts in the field, however, is the opinion of the 'native experts' – autistic individuals themselves. Despite the fact that many people with autism have tried to communicate their views and insights, these attempts have mostly passed without much professional notice, one of the reasons being that their views and insights seem unconventional to the majority of people (so-called 'normal' people).

In this book I try to show that 'different' does not mean 'abnormal' or 'defective'. 'Normalcy' is a very relative term, as the 'norm' is often applied to the performance of majority, and it is more justifiable to term it 'typical'. To avoid having to use the term 'normal', autistic people at Autism Network International, founded by Jim Sinclair and Donna Williams in 1992, have introduced a new term – 'Neurologically Typical' (NT) to describe non-autistic people.

Here I deliberately use the term 'autistic people' rather than 'people with autism' because autism is not something that is just attached to them and cannot be easily removed. I am aware of the 'people first, then disability' approach. However, without autism they would be different people, as being autistic means being different. If people with autism prefer to name themselves autistic why should we be shy to call them that? Just to show them our respect? There are other ways to do it. Autism is not something to be ashamed of. To draw a parallel, should we call Russian people as 'people from Russia' to show that we respect them despite the fact that under the communist party regime the policy of that country was, to put it mildly, incorrect.

For autistic people, autism is a way of being. It is pervasive, it colours every experience, every sensation, perception, thought, emotion – in short, every aspect of existence (Sinclair 1993). They do not respond in the way we expect them to, because they have different systems of perception and communication. Bob Morris (1999) calls it a different set of SPATS – Senses, Perceptions, Abilities and Thinking Systems – that are not in the same spectral range as NT individuals. Of course, it is very difficult to communicate with someone who uses a different 'language' (and autistic people are 'foreigners' in any culture). But it is wrong to use non-autistic methods to teach and treat autistic children. It is sure to fail and may sometimes even damage their lives.

We have to give up our conventional non-autistic assumptions and let them teach us about their communication systems in order to build bridges between the two worlds. We follow Donna Williams's recommendation of the way to help people with autism: 'If you have a camel which is finding it hard to walk under the weight of all the straws on its back, the easiest way to make it easier for the camel to walk is to take as many straws off its back as possible', and not to train '…the camel to walk or appear to walk whilst carrying the straws. To take the straws off the camel's back, you have to do two things. One is to identify them and second is to know how to remove them' (Williams 1996, p.87).

At present, as there are no known medical tests to indicate autism, the diagnosis is based on the presence of the specific behaviours (DSM-IV, ICD-10), namely impairments of social interaction, communication and imagination, known collectively as the Triad of Impairments (Wing 1992). However, these behaviours are seen as a cluster of purposeful compensatory reactions caused by some fundamental impairment(s) and cannot be considered as primary features. These behavioural charac-teristics, though very useful for diagnosis, do not tell us much about why autistic people exhibit them and how they experience the world. That is why it is no use trying to eliminate these behaviours without identifying underlying causes, no matter how much these 'bizarre reactions' interfere with teaching or treatment of autistic children.

Since Kanner's identification of autism (1943) different theories of the probable deficits in autism have emerged. Since the 1970s the main emphasis has been on the cognitive development of autistic children and different theories of cognitive deficits have been originated: 'theory of mind' (Baron-Cohen, Leslie and Frith 1985); central coherence theory (Frith 1989); executive functioning deficit theory (Ozonoff 1995) and some others. All these theories suggest that low-level perceptual processes are intact in autism and information processing up to the point of interpretation by a central system can be assumed to be normal in autism (Frith 1989).

At present it is commonly recognized that there are many possible causes of autism and some researchers distinguish several types of autism ('autisms'), all of which result in the same behavioural patterns (impairments of social interaction, communication and imagination). Though many different problems can produce similar symptoms, what defines autism is a specific combination of these problems reflected in the Triad of Impairments. There is scientific evidence that deficits in information processing, both perceptive and executive, is found in all persons within the autistic spectrum, though the role of sensory perceptual problems is still very controversial.

Although in the 1960s–70s the idea of possible sensory perceptual abnormalities as one of the core features of the disorder was put forward (Rimland 1964) and the theory of sensory dysfunction formulated (Delacato 1974), till recently it has been ignored by the researchers. What makes one wonder, is that, though unusual sensory experiences have been observed in autistic people for many years and are confirmed by autistic individuals themselves, they are still listed as an associated (and not essential) feature of autism in the main diagnostic classifications.

Although a number of works have appeared recently highlighting perceptual abnormalities in autism, to date these possible abnormalities and their role in causing autistic behaviours have not been systematically investigated. More research work is needed to find out whether perceptual problems are core features in the fundamental impairment(s) in the autistic condition, which senses are affected, the intensity with which the senses work, etc.

This book attempts to reconstruct the sensory world of autism in order to help understand the way autistic people experience the world, because very well-meaning specialists are often 'failing people with autism...[and] most [autistic people] have not been helped at all, many have felt degraded and some have been harmed' (Gerland 1998), due to misunderstanding and misinterpretation of the condition. This is the attempt to describe possible sensory experiences (not always necessarily abnormalities) based on the personal accounts of autistic people. If we can understand the causes of certain behaviours, we can accept these behaviours. If we know what to look for, it will be easier for us to understand the person's problems and abilities and to find appropriate methods to identify and remove the 'straws' from the camel. Moreover, understanding of the way autistic people experience the world will bring respect to people with autism in their attempts to survive and live a productive life in our world instead of the lack of acceptance often exhibited by the public.

What is lacking in most studies on the sensory dysfunction in autism is the opinion and views on the problem of the autistic people themselves. Bob Morris (1999) calls it 'the original error' of the investigations, i.e. trying to reconstruct the 'autistic world' using the methods and perceptions of non-autistics. To avoid this error the personal accounts and communications should be seen as the main source of information about this condition. Our approach is to listen to autistic individuals who are willing to communicate and explain how they experience the world and not to assume that only our views are right because we are specialists/parents. It is the same as if I said to you, 'Sorry, but you speak English with an accent. Let me teach you English pronunciation. It doesn't matter that I am Russian. I am a linguist so I know better than you how to speak your language properly.'

In this book the term 'types of sensory dysfunction' is replaced by the term 'types of sensory experiences', as not all the experiences turn out to be 'dysfunctional' or 'defective' but rather 'different' or 'showing super-ability' (for example, synaesthesia, 'resonance', 'daydreaming', 'acute vision/hearing' etc.) and might be considered as strengths rather than deficits.

Before we discuss the possible patterns of sensory perceptual experiences in autism it is necessary to give a brief explanation of why the role of these differences should not be ignored (Chapter 1) and to consider briefly the general concepts and issues, such as sensory systems and perception in general (Chapter 2). In Chapters 3 and 4 the possible sensory experiences and perceptual styles in autism are discussed. As sensory perceptual differences affect cognitive processes, we will further investigate how these perceptual differences are reflected in the differences of thinking (Chapter 5). Each descriptor is followed by a 'what to look for' section, to help with the identification of this particular characteristic with the 'behaviours on the surface'. Sometimes we cannot explain the behaviour because we do not know what might cause it. I hope the descriptions of the behaviours will help find the answers to some 'why does he do this' questions. While reading the descriptions and especially explanations and experiences given by the autistic authors, I would advise the reader to do two things: first, try to simulate these autistic sensory experiences in order to imagine at least what it could be like for them, and second, think of any autistic person you know. Is it about him or her? Does his or her behaviour make sense now?

Other sensory conditions, which are quite common in autism, are described in Chapter 6. The possible sensory experiences and perceptual styles are classified into 20 categories. These are by no means a complete set of the descriptors. Further research (and co-operation with autistic individuals) is needed. However, I feel, it would be a good start to achieving an understanding of a sensory world of autism.

After 'exploration' of the sensory world we move to the consideration of different treatments to eliminate sensory perceptual problems, supplemented by discussion of the limitations and strengths of different approaches and techniques addressing sensory perceptual difficulties experienced by people with autism (Chapter 7) and then to the 'rainbows' – special graphs that will help identify possible different experiences of each child in order to work with him 'on his territory' (Chapter 8). (The Sensory Profile Checklist is included at Appendix 1; it is designed to identify areas of strengths and challenge for autistic individuals.) The Sensory Perceptual Profile suggested in the book is aimed to assess the impact of these difficulties on each individual and to initiate relevant strategies and environmental changes to facilitate more effective functioning. In Chapter 9 are some ideas to help interpret the behaviours caused by sensory perceptual differences and identify the sensory perceptual difficulties of autistic individuals.

Throughout the book, examples are offered to illustrate different phenomena.

Chapter 1

Sensory Dysfunction or Different Sensory Experiences?

In recent decades, different conceptions of autism have appeared, which highlight sensory perceptual abnormalities as the basis of core features of the disorder. Some researchers describe autism as a disorder of the senses rather than a social dysfunction, where each sense operates in isolation and the brain is unable to organize the stimuli in any meaningful way (Hatch-Rasmussen 1995). It has been hypothesized that all symptoms of autism are simply a consequence of the brain injury that makes brains of autistic children perceive inputs from the world differently from non-autistic brains. Autism is sometimes defined as sensory dysfunction (Delacato 1974), a sensory integrative disorder in which the brain is not able to attach meaning to sensations and organize them into percepts and finally into concepts (Ayres 1979), etc. Unusual sensory experience is claimed by some authors to be a primary characteristic feature able to account for the basic symptoms of autism, considered to be essential according to DSM-IV and ICD-10. Thus, abnormal perceptions might give rise to high levels of anxiety, this in turn results in obsessive or compulsive behaviours, thus making the more commonly accepted criteria, in fact, secondary developmental problems (Delacato 1974).

Though, it is not as simple as that and the syndrome of autism is far too complex a phenomenon to be explained by differences in sensory experiences, sensory perceptual problems do play an important role in autism. The indirect evidence comes from the research in the fields of sensory deprivation and visual and/or auditory impairments. Sensory deprivation studies (Doman 1984) show that sudden and nearly complete deprivation of stimulation through the five senses can lead to autistic-like behaviours (withdrawal, stereotyped movements, etc.). The symptoms of sensory deprivation in animals and many autistic symptoms are similar as well: animals confined to a barren environment are excitable and engage in stereotyped behaviours and self-injury (Grandin 1996b).

The research in the field of visual impairments (Cass 1996) has shown that some similar patterns of behaviour occur in children who are blind and in those who are autistic: impairments in social interaction, communication, stereotyped movements. Gense and Gense (1994) have shown the many ways in which the behaviours of children with autism and those with visual impairments are similar. For example, such behaviours as rocking and rhythmic head banging, spinning objects, or perimeter hugging (especially in large places) and the need to touch everything in a room before settling down, are typical for both autistic and visually impaired children. In autism, this is often considered as obsessional ritual behaviour without explaining the function it serves. Autistic people argue that the original cause is of a perceptual nature. Donna Williams, a high-functioning autistic woman, for example, when asked why she does this, explained that she had difficulty perceiving herself in relation to her environment until she had done this; it gave her security by helping interpret her environment.

Common features have been also observed in the language development of children with autism and those with visual impairments, for example, echolalia and pronoun reversal – distinctive features of 'autistic language' – are also observed in the language of children with visual impairments (Fay and Schuler 1980). It is recognized that there is a critical role for visual stimulation for the development of communication. Similar 'autistic' characteristics are observed in deaf children, though in a lesser degree.

A possible explanation for this lies in the fact that around 75–80 per cent of the information about the world comes through vision, so a blind child has to make sense of or process a very different set of sensory information, which may develop emotional and psychological problems and result in 'autistic' behaviour. The researchers (Cass 1996) assume that the autistic-like picture observed in a proportion of blind children arises from the same core deficit as that in sighted autistic children. Thus, the following characteristics (Cass 1996) might be 'normal' for blind children: absence of eye contact; referential eye gaze and pointing; repetitive behaviours; language abnormalities; orienting behaviours (for instance, smelling, touching objects, etc.). There arises a question: Are autistic children 'blind' in a way, i.e. is their perception distorted?

Though blindness means there is an absence of visual information about the world, it affects all levels of functioning. To draw a parallel, one might assume autism means there are distortions of visual/auditory/ gustatory/olfactory/tactile information about the world. Whereas the blind/the deaf/the deaf-blind have other senses (that work properly) to compensate their lack of vision or hearing, and 'see' through their ears, nose and hands, or 'hear' through their hands and eyes, autistic people often cannot rely on their senses as all of them might be affected in some way.

It is worth learning how autistic individuals themselves consider the role of sensory perceptual difficulties they experience. The personal accounts of autistic individuals reveal that one of the main problems they experience is their abnormal perception, and many autistic authors consider autism as largely a condition relating to sensory processing (Gerland 1997; Grandin 1996a, b; Grandin and Scariano 1986; Lawson 1998; O'Neill 1999; Willey 1999; Williams 1992; and others). For example, J. G. T. VanDalen (1995) believes that the true invisible deep-rooted cause of all social and emotional problems is of a perceptual nature, and autism, to be really understood, has to be seen above all as a perceptual deficit. For Donna Williams (1992; 1996; 1998), her expressive difficulties were secondary and sprang from the primary inconsistencies in her perception of the world around her. Temple Grandin (1996a, b), one of the most famous autistic individuals, states that some episodes of difficult behaviour were directly caused by sensory difficulties and hypothesizes that there is a continuum of sensory processing problems for most autistic people, which goes from fractured disjointed images at one end to a slight abnormality at the other.

In the Geneva Centre for Autism (Walker and Cantello 1994) a survey was conducted to gain more insights into sensory experiences of autistic people: autistic people were asked to complete the survey anonymously through the Internet. According to the data obtained, 81 per cent of respondents reported differences in visual perception, 87 per cent in hearing, 77 per cent in tactile perception, 30 per cent in taste and 56 per cent in smell. All these data give some evidence of the possible role of distorted sensory perception in autism.

Autistic people understand that they are different in early life, but they do not know why. It is no wonder that they are often unaware that they perceive the world differently because they have nothing else to compare their perception with. Bob Morris (1999) explains: 'if you are born with different perceptions, you have no way of knowing your individual perceptions are not the same as the other 99% of the population, until your differences are called to your attention'. The first realization of the nature of their differences comes in late teens or even later. For example, it took Liane Willey, a woman with Asperger syndrome, many years before she realized that she did and thought many things that others did not, then she saw how peculiar her world was – not wrong or embarrassing or unessential – just different.

To illustrate the idea of misidentification and misunderstanding of autistic people by non-autistic individuals Bob Morris (1999) uses Hans Andersen's story 'The Ugly Duckling'. A swan egg became misplaced into a duck's nest. As it grew, it was seen as a poor performing odd duck. But in time, and after correct identification, the swan was shown to be physically more stately, majestic and powerful than any duck could even hope to be. The author concludes that if we recognize that we all have complementary, weak and strong capability patterns in our respective SPATS, the autistic person can have *life*, not *life-support*, for life. Morris's advice to professionals is to include SPATS in the diagnosis check-off and to teach the all-wise ducks how to recognize, handle and develop a swan, instead of trying to mould the swan into a defective duck. Many autistic authors emphasize that there are beneficial 'side-effects' of autism that could far outweigh the negatives (Kochmeister 1995; Grandin 1996a, 1999; O'Neill 1999; Sinclair 1992; Williams 1994).

The fact that autistic people share common systems of perception and thinking is confirmed by many autistic individuals: they report that they have very few problems communicating with and understanding people 'of their own kind' (Dekker 1999; Williams 1994). Though there are plenty of varieties in their perception, in general autistic people are no more all different than non-autistics when SPATS are considered as a whole (Morris, 1999). As the systems work differently their responses to sensory stimuli are 'normal' (from the autistic point of view), though different and unconventional, and not abnormal or defective.

It seems wrong to use non-autistic methods to treat autistic individuals. There are always two ways to look at things: the non-autistic way and the autistic way (Bovee). Our task should be to understand the second way.

In the next chapter, we briefly discuss the general concepts we will use throughout the book, namely sensory systems and perception, and compare the sensory perceptual development of autistic and non-autistic children.

Chapter 2

Perception

Sensory systems

The importance of sensory experiences is undeniable. The French philosopher, Etienne Bonnet Condillac (1715–1780) claimed that judgement, reflection and understanding originated in sensations. To illustrate the role of the senses in the shaping of the mind he described a marble statue that was given first the sense of smell, then taste, then tactility and finally hearing and vision; and the statue came to life. She generated ideas, exhibited feelings and made judgements.

To begin to understand how we sense and perceive the world, we must know how sensory mechanisms are constructed and how they operate to convey sensations, i.e. experiences caused by stimuli in the environment. The senses operate through specialized sensory organs.

Sensory organs, or receptors (organs or cells able to respond to an external stimulus such as light, heat, etc. and transmit signal to a sensory nerve), can be classified into exteroceptive (relating to stimuli produced outside an organism) and interoceptive (relating to stimuli produced within the organism) receptors. Exteroceptive sense organs are divided into distance (or far) senses (vision, hearing, olfaction) and contact (or near) senses (gustation and tactility). Interoceptive cells operate within the body, for example, proprioceptors (relating to the position and movements of the body).

Traditionally we distinguish the following sensory systems:

- vision – the faculty of seeing

- hearing – the faculty of perceiving sounds

- vestibular system – refers to structures within the inner ear that detect movement and changes in the position of the head

- olfaction (the sense of smell) – the faculty of perceiving odours or scents

- gustation (the sense of taste) – the faculty of perceiving the sensation of a soluble substance caused in the mouth and throat by contact with that substance

- tactile system – the faculty of perceiving touch, pressure, pain, temperature

- proprioceptive system – the faculty of perceiving stimuli produced within an organism, especially relating to the position and movement of the body.

Sense organs transform sensory stimuli, such as light, sounds, odours, flavours, touch, into electrical/chemical nerve signals, which are identified, put together and interpreted in the brain. The signals from each sensory organ are processed in specialized areas of the brain. Most of the sensory information (except smell) passes through the thalamus and then to the opposite hemisphere of the cortex for further processing.

Olfaction (the sense of smell)

The olfactory system is the primary sensory channel in infancy. Olfactory receptors are located in the nostrils on the olfactory epithelium and deal with odour molecules in the air. There are about 10 million smell receptors in the nose, of at least 20 different types. Each type detects a different range of smell molecules. The receptors respond quickly to minute chemicals in the air, but they also adapt to them in a very short time so that the intensity of the smell is lost very quickly. The nerve signals pass along the olfactory nerve to the smell centre in the brain that processes the electrochemical signal pattern and identifies the smell.

Smell differs from other senses in two ways. First, it is the only sense that goes straight to the amygdala (limbic system) and then to the cortex, without 'visiting' the thalamus – the central relay station from which sensory signals are transferred to regions of the cortex specialized for each sense. Second, unlike other senses, it does not go from each nostril to the opposite hemisphere but passes uncrossed to the same hemisphere.

Smell plays an important role in the way we taste.

Gustation (the sense of taste)

The receptors of taste are taste buds (taste receptors) on the tongue, inside the cheeks, on the roof of the mouth and in the throat. We have between 2000 and 5000 taste buds which are subdivided into several categories of the primary tastes: sweet (near the tip of the tongue), salty and sour (on the sides of the tongue), bitter (on the back of the tongue) and spicy. The middle of the tongue, sometimes called the tongue's blind spot, has no taste buds. The tongue can also sense temperature and texture.

The sense of taste is not very strong without the sense of smell. That is why we do not seem to feel any taste when we have a cold and our sense of smell is blocked. The senses of smell and taste are often called chemosenses because they operate in very similar ways: the sense of taste deals with chemicals in liquids and the sense of smell with chemicals in the air.

Vision

The sense organs of vision are the eyes. The function of the eyes is to receive light and let it in to the nerve endings (the sight receptors) at the back of the eyes (the retina).

The place on the retina where the nerve endings of the rods and cones form the optic nerve and its blood vessels join the retina is called the blind spot because there are no light-sensitive cells on that part of the retina and the eye does not receive light here. To find the blind spot look at one of the crosses (Figure 2.1) with one eye only. Slowly move the book towards your face. At some point, one of the crosses will seem to disappear. It is when the image falls on the blind spot.

+   +

Figure 2.1 Blind spot

Box 2.1 The eye

There are three layers of the eyeball:

- The **sclera** is the outer layer (the 'white') of the eye that protects the eyeball. The **cornea** is the transparent horny part of the anterior covering of the eyeball.

- The **choroid** is the middle layer of the eyeball, which has blood vessels and brings oxygen to the eye.

- The **retina** is the inner layer of the eye, made up of light receptors. These light receptors are of two types: **rods** and **cones**. Rods are sensitive to dim light. Cones are sensitive to bright lights and colours.

Light enters the eye through the **pupil**. The **iris** (the coloured area around the pupil) controls the amount of light entering the eye.

Directly behind the pupil is the lens. The eye's lens, like any other lens, inverts the visual image upside-down. Thus, we receive 'upside-down pictures' on the retina. It is the brain that turns them the 'right way up'.

The function of the lens is to focus the light rays. The ability of the eyes to adjust the focus by thickening or flattening of the lens is called **accommodation**. In normal sight, the light rays are focused on the retina. However, sometimes the cornea and lens do not focus correctly. In myopia (short-sightedness) light from distant objects focuses in front of the retina and images on the retina are blurred. In hypermetropia (long-sightedness) light from nearby objects focuses behind the retina and images are blurred.

Between the cornea and the lens is a jelly-like liquid called the **aqueous humour** that helps to keep the eyeball firm.

Directly behind the pupil and lens there is the **yellow spot** on the retina, where the most cones are located.

The brain learns to compensate and fill in missing parts of the image using information from the colours and shapes around it.

Each eye's visual field covers a slightly different area and each eye sees an object from a slightly different angle. The brain combines these different views of an object into one image. Seeing with two eyes is called binocular or stereoscopic vision.

Electrical signals are carried along the optic nerve from each eye and cross over at the optic chiasma, so that the signals from the right side of the left eye and the right side of the right eye go to the right hemisphere and the signals from the left side of each eye go to the left hemisphere.

The visual cortex of the brain consists of many areas, each processing different aspects of sight, such as colour, shape, size, motion, depth, distance, etc. Thus, each visual element is processed by a different brain area.

Hearing

The sense organs of hearing are the ears.

The sound information from each ear goes to the auditory cortex of the opposite hemisphere.

Vestibular system

The sense organs of balance and gravity (vestibular system) are located in the inner ear. These are three semicircular canals, covered with endolymph. These organs pass messages to the brain about movement and changes in the position of the head: when we move our head, spin, lie down, etc. the endolymph presses on the nerve endings behind the wall of each canal and sends the message to the brain.

The sense of balance is backed up by our vision and by the proprioceptors. It is much more difficult to balance on one foot with the eyes closed. When we spin, we often feel dizzy because the brain receives confusing messages about the position of the body. It takes time for babies to develop coordination between the sense of balance, sight and proprioceptors.

Box 2.2 The ear

The ear consists of three parts – the outer ear, the middle ear and the inner ear.

The outer ear

The **pinnae** (broad upper part of external ear) is used for catching and directing sound waves into the ear. The **auditory canal** is a short tube leading from the pinnae to the **eardrum** (a tightly stretched membrane closing off the outer ear). When sound waves travel down the auditory canal they make the drum vibrate. The vibrations pass along to the middle ear cavity.

The middle ear

There are three little bones – the **hammer**, the **anvil** and the **stirrup** – that form a chain across the middle ear. The vibration of the eardrum causes the vibration of these three little bones which, in turn, causes the **oval window** (another membrane in the inner ear at the opposite side from the eardrum) to vibrate.

The **Eustachian tube** is a passage communicating between the middle ear and the back of the throat (larynx), and serving to equalize air-pressure on both sides of the eardrum.

The inner ear

The vibration of the oval window causes the **perilymph** (a fluid in the inner ear) to vibrate and to produce the vibration in the **endolymph** (a fluid surrounding auditory nerve endings) and send electrochemical information along the auditory receptors to the brainstem and through the thalamus to the auditory cortex of the temporal lobe for further processing.

Proprioception

The proprioceptive system (kinaesthetic sense) receives the information from contracting and stretching muscles, bending and compression of joints, and provides awareness of body position. Receptors in muscles, tendons and joints inform the brain about the position and posture of the body. Proprioceptors also identify the right amount of pressure to pick up something light or heavy.

Proprioceptive information is processed in many different brain areas.

Tactility

The sense of touch is one of the first senses to develop; it develops in the uterus. The sense of tactility plays an important role in receiving information about the environment and in exhibiting protective reactions.

The sense organ of tactility is skin. There are five different types of tactile receptors in the different skin layers: for light touch, for pressure, for pain, for heat and for cold.

Different types of touch receptors respond to different kinds of stimuli. For example, Pacini's endings respond mainly to pressure; Merkel's and Meissner's endings react to touch and small, fast vibrations; Ruffini's endings detect changes in temperature and pressure; nociceptors are primary receptors of pain caused by extreme temperature, pressure and so on.

Millions of tactile receptors are scattered all over the skin, more highly packed in some places, for example, the fingertips, making them very sensitive, and with less density in others, for instance, the back. When tactile receptors are stimulated by touch, heat, cold or vibration they send the signals to the special areas in the brain.

When we get dressed we can feel our clothes on the skin, but then the feeling fades. This fading of sensation is called habituation. It is the same with smell and taste. If the senses are exposed to a continuing stimulus, habituation soon occurs. When the stimulus changes, the feeling returns. Like with smell and taste, tactile receptors display habituation to a continuous stimulus. That is why we do not feel the clothes we are wearing and become aware of them only if we change or adjust them.

What is perception?

Everything we know about the world and ourselves has come through our senses. All our knowledge therefore is the product of what we have seen, heard, smelt, etc. The process by which an organism collects, interprets and comprehends information from the outside world by means of senses is called perception. The process of perception has several stages. It starts with sensation. This is an elementary process incapable of analysis; it takes no account of any external object, being simply feeling. Sensations possess quality, intensity and duration. They may be broadly divided into affective (pleasure, pain) and representative (taste, touch, smell, heat). At the level of the perceptual (literal and objective), there is no understanding that things can have meaning beyond what is perceptually available (Powell 2000).

Once the incoming information has passed through special areas in the brain the sensory perceptions are joined with appropriate cognitive associations and are bound to general types of things in memory (concepts). For example, the perception of a pen is joined with the concept of writing:

Stimulus $\longrightarrow$	Sensation $\longrightarrow$	Interpretation $\longrightarrow$ (Percept)	Comprehension (Concept)
A pen $\longrightarrow$ (an object)	A long thin $\longrightarrow$ cylindrical plastic thing	A pen $\longrightarrow$	I can write with it

Sensory perceptual development

A baby is not born with knowledge and strategies ready-made for perceiving the complexities of environmental stimuli. This ability develops with age. After birth, the baby's interaction with the environment immediately becomes a source of knowledge. Infants acquire information about the world and constantly check the validity of that information; the process defines perception: extracting information from stimulation (Gibson 1969).

Perception depends on both learning and maturation. Babies are not given the perceptual world with all its categories at birth. They actively create it through their experiences, memories and cognitive processes. For babies, even their own body does not exist as a whole, rather as 'separate organs such as hands, mouth, arms and belly' and they know 'nothing of the various parts being related together' (Tustin 1974, p.60). Gradually babies learn to 'feel self' and control their body parts to produce meaningful movements.

The baby has to learn how to see, to hear, etc. Thus, vision or hearing means the ability to receive sights or sounds, but this ability does not include comprehending visual images and sounds. We have to learn how to see and hear with meaning. We develop our visual and auditory processing skills and achieve the comprehension through interaction with the environment. Babies are learning how to discriminate different stimuli from a chaos of sounds, shapes, patterns, movements, and in the first months of their lives infants achieve the ability to make fine discriminations between the slightest variations in colour, form, sound, etc. Babies also have to learn how to get and store the information from their senses. They actually *learn* how to use their sensory organs and connect sensory images with meanings.

If the perceptual processes are functioning appropriately, the infant is able to 'make sense' out of the environment. On the other hand, distorted sensory input becomes distorted information (Ornitz 1983; 1985). If one (or several) of the senses is lost (for example, sight or hearing), the other senses develop to compensate and create the balance. However, the sensory perceptual worlds of blind or deaf people are very different from the sensory perceptual world of people without these disabilities. It is not enough to shut the eyes or ears to imagine how they experience life. Here we can talk about different perceptions, different languages, and even different cultures.

For example, the blind live in a tactile/auditory/olfactory/gustatory world without any visual perceptions. Their experiences are based on their interaction with the world through the senses available to them. This is by no means a dysfunctional world. It is rather a completely different world. Instead of visual images, they have tactile-motor concepts. Their perception of space and time is different. They perceive distance by time – by how long it has taken to reach or pass objects. The blind compensate the lack of vision by other senses (often very acute) and reconstruct their 'visionless' world rich in sound images, tactile and olfactory 'pictures' that is very difficult for sighted people even to imagine.

In his book *An Anthropologist on Mars*, Oliver Sacks writes about a man named Virgil who had been blind for 45 years. When his sight was restored, the results were very surprising (and in many ways disappointing). Virgil could see but he could not interpret what he saw. He was still 'blind' to the meaning of visual stimuli. He could reach the 'visual meaning' if he touched the objects, i.e. using his tactile system. He could 'see' with his ears, nose or hands much better than with his eyes. He had to learn to connect visual experiences with meaning. As his world had been built up with other senses, Virgil had great difficulty in learning how to use his eyes – he would attend visually only if he was asked to. Without visual experience and visual memory, he had problems recognizing objects, animals or people. He could not even distinguish between a circle and a square if he was not allowed to touch them. Virgil was 'mentally blind' – able to see but not to decipher what he was seeing (Sacks 1995). Extraneous information that came through his eyes that was not backed up with visual experiences and visual memories brought only confusion into his perception. This 'foreign' information interfered with his ability to interpret the environment. He could 'see' better without his eyes!

Problems similar to Virgil's may be experienced by congenitally deaf people whose hearing is restored later in life. Initially they find themselves in the world of chaotic sounds, which they are unable to interpret ('mentally deaf'). It takes them a long time to learn to use their ears and attach meaning to auditory images. They have to learn to 'translate' auditory stimuli into visual/olfactory ones in order to learn their meaning. Those whose vision or hearing is restored at a younger age, have fewer problems with adjustment to their new perceptual world. Thus, the timing when perceptual problems are handled is very important.

Some autistic children may require to be taught how to see using their eyes, how to hear using their ears, how to eat and how to move. Jim Sinclair (1992), a high-functioning person with autism, emphasizes that simple, basic skills such as recognizing people and things presuppose even simpler, more basic skills such as knowing how to attach meaning to visual stimuli. Understanding speech requires knowing how to process sounds, that, in turn first requires recognizing sounds as things that can be processed, and recognizing processing as a way to extract order from chaos. Autistic individuals may experience problems acquiring these skills. More complex functions such as speech (or any kind of motor behaviour) require the ability to keep track of all the body parts involved, and to coordinate all their movements. Producing any behaviour in response to any perception requires monitoring and coordinating all the inputs and outputs at once, and doing it fast enough to keep up with changing inputs that may call for changing outputs (Sinclair 1992). Autistic children do not seem to possess these basic, taken for granted by us, abilities.

So how do we learn to use our senses in order to make sense of the world around us? Eleanor Gibson (1969) identifies three trends in perceptual development:

1. *Increasing specificity of discrimination.* Maturing organisms restrict their reactions to a stimulus, i.e. they respond only to the true stimulus or a close approximation. Youngsters show a steady increase in the precision and consistency of their discriminations and they also manifest a constant reduction in the time needed to discriminate.

2. *The optimization of attention.* Perception is an active process that changes developmentally. Children of the early childhood age are vigorously active, and their perceptual processes are now more searching than the passive perceptual responses of infancy: their eye movements, for example, no longer fixate on a single spot of an object but follow its contour seeking distinctive features. They select needed information from complex stimuli, thus demonstrating attention to relevant and disregarding irrelevant stimuli. Changes in ability to attend to wanted information and ignore the irrelevant occur with age.

3. *Increasing economy in information pickup.* Combining the first two of these developmental trends helps to explain growing perceptual sophistication. Youngsters learn to discriminate an object by focusing on the fewest possible features that distinguish it. If they can isolate some invariant, i.e. a feature that remains constant over time, they have drastically improved their perception of an object. They thus increase their ability to

process several objects or events simultaneously because they see relationships and can form structures, which facilitates retention and economical recall.

The real world and the perceived world (i.e. our mental image of the world) differ. All the information we receive from our senses is constructed (pieced together) in our brain. Our brain cannot process all the stimuli present; therefore, it selects the key aspects of the scene while the rest of the world falls into the background. That is, the process of perception is an active process, guided by the brain. Moreover, it is a two-way process: information from the sense organs (relatively raw material) is influenced by the 'inside information' (the information we have stored and adjusted to our earlier experiences).

What is more, with age we often tend to 'distort' what we perceive even more because we often add to our perception by 'seeing', 'hearing', etc. what we *expect* to see, hear, etc. in certain situations. These expectations are based on our experience and knowledge. We do not have to examine the flat vertical surface with a handle every time we see it, to know that this is a door and we can open it to get into the house. A lot of 'perceptual constancies' stored in our brain help us to move in our world with confidence and certainty and 'save the time' for other cognitive processes (solving problems, planning activities, etc.).

Our interpretation ('seeing') of the world is based on our imagination, memory and experience. For instance, we know from our past experience the size of objects and people. We use this knowledge to 'see' and interpret things and people we are confronted with at present. As a result, the final picture (multi-sensory: visual, auditory, olfactory, etc.) is inevitably distorted, without our even realizing that our 'perceived world' is not a true copy of the real one. Looking at the three people in the picture (Figure 2.2), we *know* that the person who is farthest away should look smaller. If this person looks of the same height, we interpret it as if he or she is the tallest even though the three of them are exactly the same. This is an example of visual illusion. However, we may experience illusions in any sensory modality.

Illusion is defined as erroneous interpretation of something really existent and actually perceived by the senses. Some illusions arise from imperfect knowledge or perception, others from a disordered condition of

Figure 2.2 Which person is the tallest?

Figure 2.3 A vase or two faces?

the senses, as when someone sees two objects where one exists. In contrast to hallucinations, illusions are errors of perception and/or construction, rather than false constructions (Carter 1998).

We may distinguish several types of illusions:

1. Illusions caused by some physiological and/or mechanical processes, for example, blind spot; the halo effect (when brightness persists after bright light has been switched off due to residual firing of the light receptors in the retina).

2. Illusions caused by 'filtering foreground and background information', when our perception depends on what we have picked as a foreground image, for example, a vase or two faces (see Figure 2.3).

3. Cognitive illusions – caused by cognitive interpretation of the perceived stimuli, for example, when we 'see' what we expect to see.

'Seeing' or 'not seeing' visual illusions provides an objective and replicable way of examining visual-constructive capacities of the brain (Sacks 1995). Oliver Sacks quotes the case of S.B., a blind person whose vision was restored when he was in his fifties. S.B.'s responses to visual illusions were very peculiar. 'Physiological illusions', such as parallel lines that seem to diverge because of the effect of diverging lines on them, were seen as parallel by him. Reversing figures ('filtering illusions'), such as cubes and staircases drawn in perspective or ambiguous figures, did not reverse for S.B. and were not seen in depth. He had no 'figure-ground fluctuation' and saw one 'image' without changing from foreground to background perspective. Sacks interprets S.B.'s failure to 'see' the illusion as evidence of rudimentary visual constructions and absence of early visual experience.

Thus, there is always something of *us* in our interpretation of stimuli. Our response is not objective. It depends on our previous experiences, interests, motivation, etc. Besides, our perception is also influenced by our culture. And though every brain constructs the world in a slightly different way from any other because every brain is different, the ways it operates are similar for non-disabled people. Even with perceptual differences, we see sufficient similarity to agree that a book is a book, a cat is a cat, etc.

Chapter 3

Possible Sensory Experiences in Autism

What is the autistic way to perceive the world?

> Learning how each individual autistic person's senses function is one crucial key to understanding that person. (O'Neill 1999, p.31)

Though autistic people live in the same physical world and deal with the same 'raw material', their perceptual world turns out to be strikingly different from that of non-autistic people. It is widely reported that autistic people have unusual (from a non-autistic point of view) sensory perceptual experiences. These experiences may involve hyper- or hyposensitivity, fluctuation between different 'volumes' of perception, difficulty interpreting a sense, etc. All these experiences are based on real experiences, like those of non-autistic people, but these experiences may look/sound/feel, etc. different, or they may be interpreted differently. We think about the world in a way we experience it and perceive it to be. Different experience brings a different stock of knowledge about the world. So can we be sure that we are moving in the same perceptual/social, etc. world if our reconstructions of it are so different? Can we be sure that we see, hear, feel, etc. exactly the same things? How can we know that only our 'perceptual version' of the world is correct and theirs is wrong? Whatever the answer to these questions it is worth remembering that autistic people cannot help seeing and hearing the 'wrong thing', and they do not even know that they see or hear the wrong thing (Rand). 'Normal' connections between things and events do not make sense for them, but may be overwhelming, confusing and scary.

What makes the matter even more complicated is that no two autistic people appear to have the exactly same patterns of sensory perceptual experiences.

We can distinguish some features of 'autistic perception' of the world, based on the testimonies of high-functioning autistic individuals and close observation of autistic children. Below we will discuss the most commonly reported perceptual phenomena.

These experiences are not unique. We all may 'feel strange' sometimes and have similar experiences now and then, especially when tired or drugged. What is unique about these experiences in autism is their intensity and continuity: these experiences are 'normal' for them.

'Literal perception'

> Most things I take at face value, without judging or interpreting them. I look at them in a concrete, literal, and very individual way. I do not normally integrate things or see them as connected unless I actively look for a connection. I do not 'draw' connections, I assign them consciously, based on reasoning and usefulness. All my associations are consciously formed, and may be consciously severed. (Blackburn 1999, p.10)

Autistic people seem to perceive everything as it is. It is sort of 'literal perception', for example, they may *see* things without interpretation and understanding (literal vision). Professor Snyder, who studies the phenomenon of autistic savants, suggests that autistic people look at the world the way it actually is.

A very good example of our inability to actually see the world the way it is without the brain's interference with the process is the way we interpret so-called impossible objects. Looking at the top part of the figure (Figure 3.1), we interpret it as a construction with two columns. However, if we change the perspective and look at the bottom, we 'change our mind' and conclude that there are three columns. As we *know* that this is impossible (though our eyes tell us the opposite), we arrive at the conclusion that this is an impossible object.

Figure 3.1 Impossible object

Inability to distinguish between foreground and background information ('Gestalt perception')

> It was like having a brain with no sieve… (Williams 1994, p.42)

There is much evidence that one of the problems many autistic people experience is their inability to distinguish between foreground and background stimuli (inability to filter foreground and background information). They often are unable to discriminate relevant and irrelevant stimuli (Gibson's first two stages of perceptual development). What is background to others may be equally foreground to them; they perceive everything without filtration or selection. It is often hard for the autistic person to integrate what they are experiencing into separate and unique entities (Joan and Rich 1999), to 'break' the whole picture into meaningful parts.

Delacato (1974) discovered that some autistic children ('hypervisual' in his classification) are not fooled by optical illusions and identified it as one on the visual 'isms'. Several theories have appeared trying to explain the phenomenon of 'optical disillusions' in autism: the theory of 'probable prediction' (Feigenberg 1986) and the modification of the 'weak central coherence theory' (Frith 1989) to low levels (Happe 1996).

Feigenberg (1986) suggests that what we see (hear, feel, etc.) is mostly something we are expecting to see (hear, feel, etc.). The brain does not need to process all the stimuli; it just 'fills in the gaps' and 'predicts' the final picture. That is why we are prone to illusions. This ability of the brain to 'see' before actually seeing is not restricted to vision. The same can be observed with other senses, for example, we can 'hear' or 'feel' what we are expecting to hear or feel.

Happe (1996) interprets low susceptibility to illusions in autistic individuals as evidence of weak central coherence, as visual illusions require processing of information in context, i.e. holistically. If autistic people perceive everything in fragments and focus on these fragments without integrating them with the surrounding illusion-inducing context, one might expect them to succumb less to the typical misperceptions (Happe 1996). A recent study (Garner and Hamilton 2001), however, has questioned the proposition of universal weak central coherence in autistic people. Garner and Hamilton (2001) demonstrated that some autistic individuals (all nine autistic participants in their study) are able to experience visual illusions and implement central coherence, and some of the participants experienced it even before the non-autistic ones. The researchers conclude that the idea that weak central coherence dominates all perceptual experience of autistic individuals is incorrect.

The results of the study of Ozonoff *et al.* (1994) have also questioned the weak central coherence in autism. They reveal that the autistic group demonstrated no particular difficulty processing global features of a stimulus, nor did they exhibit superiority in processing local features, relative to the two matched control groups, one with Tourette syndrome and the other developmentally normal. Ozonoff *et al.* (1994) hypothesize that autistic individuals do indeed focus on details at the expense of seeing the big picture, but do this at a conceptual, rather than a perceptual level. That is, they may have no trouble visually processing the whole picture; difficulty may only be apparent when the individual elements are meaningful pieces of information that must be integrated to form a general idea or understanding at a higher-order conceptual level.

The inability to filter foreground and background information can account for both strengths and weaknesses of autistic perception. On the one hand, they seem to perceive more accurate information and a larger amount of it. On the other hand, this amount of unselected information cannot be processed simultaneously and may lead to information overload. As Donna Williams describes it, they seem to have no sieves in their brains to select the information that is worth being attended to. This results in a paradoxical phenomenon: sensory information is received in infinite detail and holistically at the same time. It can be described as 'gestalt perception'[1], i.e. perception of the whole scene as a single entity with all the details perceived (not processed!) simultaneously. They may be aware of the information others miss, but the processing of 'holistic situations' can be overwhelming.

The phenomenon of autistic savants can contribute a lot to the explanation of 'autistic perception'. Steven Wiltshire, a well-known autistic artist, for example, draws pictures of architectural buildings with minute detail. It has been suggested that this ability is the result of photographic memory that helps hold the whole scene together. Another interesting feature of his drawings is that he could start the picture from any (often insignificant) detail and complete it with ease. Could it be that for him all these details are one entity? If you want to draw a circle, you can start from any point and complete it. For people like Steven, who perceive the gestalt, the starting point does not matter, as for us it does not matter from what point we start to draw a circle.

Louis, an autistic boy (aged nine at the time) completed his picture of Humpty Dumpty in ten minutes after having watched a cartoon (Figure 3.2).

Many autistic children, whose drawings though are not so spectacular, exhibit the same technique of creating a picture. They may start to draw a car with a wheel, a man with a foot, etc. Gestalt perception may account for their 'superability' to see simultaneously two pictures in one (for example, well-known 'vase-faces' picture). Other 'disillusions' (for example, Titcher circles, etc.) can be accounted for by 'probable prediction' deficit (Feigenberg 1986).

Gestalt perception is often overwhelming and may lead to all sorts of distortions during the processing of information, such as fragmented

Figure 3.2 'Humpty Dumpty'. Drawing by Louis, aged nine years old

perception, hypersensitivity, fluctuation between hyper- and hyposensitivity, delayed processing, etc.

It is common knowledge that autistic people do not like changes and like routines. If a slightest detail is changed (for example, a picture on the wall is not straight, or a piece of furniture has been moved a few inches to the side), the whole scene (gestalt) is different, i.e. unfamiliar. For them to recognize things, things must be exactly the same as they have already experienced. Only then will they know what to do with them (Williams 1996). The same is true about routines: if something goes differently, they do not know what to do. The gestalt of the situation is different.

All this results in fear, stress and frustration.

Paradoxically, autistic people have much more trouble with slight changes than with big ones. For instance, they can cope with going somewhere unfamiliar much better than with changes in the arrangement of the furniture in their room. The explanation of this phenomenon lies in the gestalt perception. Their encounter with new information is a new gestalt, which will be stored, while any changes in the 'familiar gestalt' bring confusion: on the one hand, it becomes a complete 'new picture', on the other hand, in the familiar situation they are confronted with an unfamiliar environment.

Autistic people may experience gestalt perception in any sensory modality. A person who experiences visual gestalt has a great difficulty focusing on a single detail of the scene and finds it almost impossible to separate it from the whole picture. People with auditory gestalt perception have a great difficulty to concentrating on one auditory stimulus, for example, someone's voice as it goes as a package with all the environmental noises: fans working, doors opening, somebody coughing, cars passing, etc. Their ears seem to pick up all sounds with equal intensity. If they try to screen out the background noise (separate it from the voice they want to attend to), they also screen out the voice they are trying to attend. The same problem occurs when several people are talking at once: it is difficult for them to listen to one voice and screen out the others (Grandin 1996b). They often feel 'drowned' in the 'sea of background noise' and cannot isolate the words of the person they are talking to from those talking within the room, in the next room, outside, etc. In crowded places, their brains seem to try to process all the stimuli around them – what every other person is saying, and what other noises and sounds coming from all directions mean.

What to look for:

1   Is not fooled by optical illusions

2   Notices every tiny change in the environment

3   Does not recognize a familiar environment if approached from a different direction

4   Gets easily frustrated when trying to do something in a noisy, crowded room

5   Does not seem to understand the instructions if more than one person is talking

6   Is unable to distinguish between tactile stimuli of different intensity (e.g. light and rough touch)

7   Is unable to distinguish between strong and weak odours/tastes

8   Clumsy; moves stiffly

9   Resists change to head position/movement

> *Alex notices every tiny change in the environment ('The rubber is under the table' 'The picture is not straight', etc.). I should be very careful about these changes, as the boy would not do anything unless he 'puts everything right'; i.e. the way it used to be.*

Brad Rand, a high-functioning person with autism gives very good examples to illustrate this phenomenon:

> You seem to learn general things, like shirts hanging in a closet, then you can process little changes about those things easily and quickly, like the shirts are still shirts hanging in a closet no matter what order they're in, or if one has fallen off its hanger a little, or if pants have accidentally got mixed into the shirts.
>
> But some people who are different learn specific things, like when they learn about shirts hanging in a closet, they learn those exact shirts in that exact order. Anything different that they see next time is not what they learned. Maybe it is like kids who learn to read by memorizing the shapes of letters, instead of by phonics. They can read Sat because they learned s and a and t equal Sat. But they can't read Cat, because the c changes everything. (Rand, pp.12–13)

As there is too much information coming in, it is hard to know which stimuli to attend to. As the stock of knowledge accumulated by autistic individuals is different, then their attention would also be different.

Here arises the question: Does the explanation of 'gestalt perception' contradict the 'weak central coherence theory' (Frith 1989) in autism? No, it does not. The theory of weak central coherence 'starts working' at the next stage of the process of perception when gestalt perception inevitably leads to distortions and fragmentation, in order to limit the amount of information to be processed.

Different stages (and styles) of perception can account for the controversial findings of the studies investigating weak central coherence and global processing in autism. On the one hand, Embedded Figures

Tests have been considered as the strongest area where autistic individuals perform better than non-autistic ones (Joliffe and Baron-Cohen 1997; Shah and Frith 1993) and the results have been interpreted as an illustration of weak central coherence in autism. On the other hand, the recent study (Garner and Hamilton 2001) has challenged this idea and shown that autistic individuals can see optical illusions, i.e. have the ability to cohere. The authors interpret these findings as the confirmation of Happe's (1999) notion about coherence being a continuum and representing a cognitive style. Whether it is a cognitive style or a perceptual style, we cannot talk about a continuum here, as one and the same person seems to be able to display both styles at different times. Thus the overflow of sensory information that cannot be filtered and/or processed simultaneously may cause distortions in perception.

Gestalt perception may result in different sensory experiences and compensatory strategies (voluntary and involuntary) the person acquires in order to cope with sensory information overload.

Most commonly reported sensory experiences in autism are:

- hypersensitivity and/or hyposensitivity
- disturbance by certain stimuli and/or fascination by certain stimuli
- inconsistency of perception (fluctuation between hyper- and hyposensitivity)
- fragmented perception
- distorted perception
- sensory agnosia (difficulty interpreting a sense)
- delayed perception
- sensory overload.

Hypersensitivity and/or hyposensitivity

In his book *The Ultimate Stranger: The Autistic Child*, describing possible sensory problems in autism, Carl Delacato (1974) classified each sensory channel as being:

- *hyper-*: the channel is too open, as a result too much stimulation gets in for the brain to handle

- *hypo-*: the channel is not open enough, as a result too little of the stimulation gets in and the brain is deprived

- '*white noise*': the channel creates its own stimulus because of its faulty operation and, as a result the message from the outside world is overcome by the noise within the system.

Delacato stated that each sensory channel could be affected in a different way, for example, a child could be hypovisual, 'white noise' auditory, hypo- to tastes and smells and hypertactile.

While recognizing the revolutionary contribution to the understanding of autism made by Delacato, it seems necessary to argue one point in his theory. Delacato considered that a channel could be either hyper- or hypo- or 'white noise'. However, it turns out that often one and the same person can experience sensory inputs of one and the same channel at different times from all three of Delacato's categories – hyper-, hypo-, 'white noise' – because the intensity (the volume) with which the channels work often fluctuates. For example, an autistic boy in my group can watch 'spots' and 'moths' (small particles in the air), shows great discomfort at bright lights (Delacato's characteristics of being hypervisual), while he often inspects objects by hand, likes mirrors (hypovisual) and has large pupils, often looks through people and things, dislikes eye contact and has distorted visual experience ('white noise').

While describing their unusual sensory experiences autistic individuals prefer the term 'hypersensitivity'. This term is very broad. In this book 'hypersensitivity' means acute or heightened, or excessive sensitivity; 'hyposensitivity' stands for below normal sensitivity. Here the terms are deliberately narrowed, as it seems more justifiable to distinguish between different sensory experiences, often conventionally covered by one term. Below are some examples of hyper- and hyposensitivities of all the channels experienced by autistic individuals.

Hypersensitivity

Hypervision (seeing 'invisible') means that they can see more than other people, i.e. their vision is too acute. For example, Alex, an autistic child, often complains 'Moths [air particles] are flying.' His vision is so hypersensitive that 'moths' often become a background with the rest of his environment fading away. Annabel Stehli (1991, p.186) described her autistic daughter Georgiana who saw 'too well' and everything she saw was magnified; 'she saw like an eagle'; she saw, for example, every strand of hair 'like spaghetti...[that] must have been why she'd been so fascinated by people's hair'. Jasmine O'Neill (1999) describes an autistic person as the person who sees what is around him with extra-acute sight.

Hyperhearing (hearing 'inaudible') is widely reported. Temple Grandin (1996b) describes her hearing as having a sound amplifier set on maximum loudness, and she compares her ears with a microphone that picks up and amplifies sounds. They might be able to hear some frequencies that only animals normally hear (Williams 1992). Alex, an autistic boy, seems to hear noises before other people. He can announce his dad coming home before anybody else can hear the car turning to the porch. As noises seem so much louder to him, Alex usually moves away from conversations and avoids crowded places.

Children with hyperhearing often cover their ears when the noise is painful for them, though others in the same room may be unaware of any disturbing sounds at all.

Hypertaste/Hypersmell: Some autistic individuals have olfactory sensitivities comparable to canines (Morris 1999). For them, 'almost all types of food smell too sharp' and they 'cannot tolerate' how people smell, even if they are very clean. They do not like some food because 'the smell or taste' might be intolerable (Rand). Hypersensitivity to certain stimuli experienced by autistic people can be compared with allergies (O'Neill 1999). Donna Williams's allergic reaction to some perfumes made the inside of her nose feel like it had been walled up with clay up to her eyebrows, some perfumes 'burned her lungs' (Williams 1996).

Some food problems, however, may be caused not by taste or smell but by intolerance of textures of certain food, sounds it produces or even its colour. Alex, for example, would never eat any red vegetables or fruit. He would accept a green apple but never a red one!

Hypertactility is very common among the autistic population. Some autistic children pull away when people try to hug them, because they fear being touched. Many children refuse to wear certain clothes, as they cannot tolerate the texture on their skin. Because their hypertactility results in overwhelming sensations, even the slightest touch can send them to a panic attack. Small scratches that most people ignore can be very painful to them. Parents often report that washing their child's hair or cutting nails turns into an ordeal demanding several people to complete it. Luke Jackson (2002), a teenager with Asperger syndrome, describes his autistic brother Ben who has real problems with clothes. Ben will now wear his clothes to go out to school, but as soon as he comes home he cannot help stripping them off – 'Hurts!'

For some people it takes many days to stop feeling their clothes on their body. And unfortunately, when this comfortable feeling (or 'non-feeling') has been achieved it is time to wear clean ones, so the process of getting used to it starts again.

Gillingham (1991) states that this 'superability' of autistic people, when the senses are so finely tuned that they make them acutely aware of things the 'normal' person would not notice, sometimes causes extreme pain. The researcher hypothesizes that to block this pain the body produces endomorphins that, in turn, may suppress further sensory information.

Temple Grandin (2000) suggests that a partial explanation for the lack of empathy in autism may be due to an oversensitive nervous system that prevents an autistic child from receiving comforting tactile stimulation from being hugged.

Vestibular hypersensitivity is reflected in a low tolerance for any activity that involves movement or quick change in the position of the body. People with vestibular hypersensitivity experience difficulty changing direction and are poor at sports. They feel disoriented after spinning, jumping or running. They often express fear and anxiety of having their feet leave the ground. Ayres (1979) termed them 'gravitationally insecure'.

Proprioceptive hypersensitivity is reflected in odd body posturing, difficulty manipulating small objects, etc.

Hyposensitivity

There might be times when they are not getting enough information, then their brain can feel empty and stop processing and they do not really see anything or hear anything. They are just there. Then they might get the information going again in their brain and nervous system by waving their hands around or rocking back and forth or making strange sounds or hitting their head with their hand (Rand).

Hypovision: Some autistic people may experience trouble figuring out where objects are, as they see just outlines, and even bright lights are not 'bright enough' for them. They may stare at the sun for a long time, or walk around something, running their hand around the edges so they can understand what it is (Rand).

Hypohearing: We often see children who 'seek sounds' (leaning their ear against electric equipment or enjoying crowds, sirens). They often create sounds themselves to stimulate their hearing – banging doors, tapping things, vocalizing.

Hypotaste/Hyposmell: Children with hypotaste/hyposmell chew and smell everything they can get – grass, play dough, perfume.

Hypotactility: Those with hypotactility seem not to feel pain or temperature. They may not notice a wound caused by a sharp object or may seem unaware of a broken bone.

Vestibular hyposensitivity: They enjoy and seek all sorts of movement and can spin or swing for a long time without being dizzy or nauseated. Autistic people with vestibular hyposensitivity often rock forth and back or move in circles while rocking their body.

Proprioceptive hyposensitivity: They have difficulty knowing where their bodies are in space; are often unaware of their own body sensations (for instance, they do not feel hunger). Children with hypoproprioceptive systems appear floppy, often lean against people, furniture and walls.

Delacato (1974) was one of the first researchers to suggest that hyper- and hyposensitivity experienced by autistic children caused all autistic behaviours, namely withdrawal from social interaction and communication, stereotypic behaviours (or stims, or self-stimulations). He called these behaviours sensoryisms (sensorisms: blindisms – visual 'isms', deafisms – auditory 'isms', etc.) and considered them as the child's attempts to treat himself and either normalize his sensory channels or communicate his problems.

Autistic individuals often describe their stims as defensive mechanisms from hyper- or hyposensitivity. Sometimes they engage in these behaviours to suppress the pain or calm themselves down (in the case of hypersensitivity), sometimes to arouse the nervous system and get sensory stimulation from the outside (in the case of hyposensitivity), and sometimes to provide themselves with internal pleasure. Very often, therefore, these self-stimulatory behaviours ('sensorisms'), which are defined by non-autistic people as 'bizarre behaviours' (such as rocking, spinning, flapping their hands, tapping fingers, watching things spin), can be viewed as involuntary strategies the child has acquired to cope with 'unwelcome stimulation' (hypersensitivity) or lack of it (hyposensitivity). That is why, no matter how irritating and meaningless these behaviours may seem to us, it is unwise to stop them without learning the function they serve and introducing experiences with the same function. The stereotypies caused by sensory hyper- or hyposensitivity can involve one or all senses. If we interpret these behaviours, we will be able to imagine (if not fully comprehend) how the child perceives the world and help the child develop strategies to cope with these (often painful) sensitivities.

In order to recognise the presence of hyper- or hyposensitivities, one should know what signs to look for. Below are some common signs indicating the sensitivities in each sensory channel that can be helpful in compiling a child's sensory perceptual profile and choosing the methods and environments suitable for each child.

What to look for:

Hyper-

Hypo-

Vision

Hyper-

- constantly looks at minute particles, picks up smallest pieces of dust
- dislikes dark and bright lights
- is frightened by sharp flashes of light, lightning, etc.
- looks down most of the time
- covers or closes eyes at bright light

Hypo-

- is attracted to light
- looks intensely at objects or people
- moves fingers or objects in front of the eyes
- is fascinated with reflections, bright coloured objects
- runs a hand around the edge of the object
- perimeter hugging

Hearing

Hyper-

- covers ears
- is a very light sleeper
- is frightened by animals
- dislikes thunderstorm, sea, crowds, etc.
- dislikes haircut
- avoids sounds and noises
- makes repetitive noises to block out other sounds

Hypo-

- bangs objects, doors
- likes vibration
- likes kitchen, bathroom
- likes crowds, traffic, etc.
- tears paper, crumples paper in his hand
- is attracted by sounds, noises
- makes loud rhythmic noises

Hyper-   **Hypo-**

Tactility

- resists being touched
- cannot tolerate new clothes; avoids wearing shoes
- overreacts to heat/cold/pain
- avoids getting 'messy'
- dislikes food of certain texture
- avoids people

- likes pressure, tight clothes
- seeks pressure by crawling under heavy objects
- hugs tightly
- enjoys rough and tumble play
- prone to self-injuries
- low reaction to pain and temperature

Smell

- toileting problems
- runs from smells
- wears the same clothes
- moves away from people

- smells self, people and objects
- smears (plays with) faeces
- seeks strong odours
- bedwetting

Taste

- poor eater
- uses tip of tongue for tasting
- gags/vomits easily
- craves certain foods

- eats anything (pica)
- mouths and licks objects
- eats mixed food (e.g. sweet and sour)
- regurgitates

Hyper-   **Hypo-**

Proprioception

| | |

- places body in strange positions
- difficulty manipulating small objects (e.g. buttons)
- turns the whole body to look at something

- low muscle tone
- has a weak grasp; drops things
- a lack of awareness of body position in space
- unaware of their own body sensations (e.g. does not feel hunger, etc.)
- bumps into objects, people
- appears floppy, often leans against people, furniture, walls
- stumbles frequently; has tendency to fall
- rocks back and forth

Vestibular

- fearful reactions to ordinary movement activities (e.g. swings, slides, merry-go-round round, etc.)
- difficulty with walking or crawling on uneven or unstable surfaces
- dislikes head upside down
- Becomes anxious or distressed when feet leave the ground

- enjoys swings, merry-go-round
- spins, runs round and round
- rocks back and forth

In my class there are four children suffering from hyper- or hyposensitivities:

Alex's vision is very acute (hyper-): he can see the tiniest particles in the air, the smallest pieces of fluff on the carpet. These experiences distract his attention from whatever he is supposed to do. He hates bright lights and fluorescent light gives him headaches. What makes things even more complicated is that Alex's hearing is also very acute. He can hear what is going on in the next room but one and always keeps me informed about it – 'The chair is being moved. The ruler has been dropped. The bus is coming', etc.

Helen's vision is hypo-: she is attracted by any shining object, looks intensely at people (that irritates Alex, who cannot tolerate any direct look at him), is fascinated with mirrors. At the lessons she can move her fingers in front of her face for hours. It seems she cannot get enough visual stimulation and always switches on all the lights as soon as she enters the classroom. (This is usually followed by a fight with Alex who throws a tantrum every time the light is on.) Helen's hearing is also hypo-: she cannot tolerate silence, and if there is not enough noise for her, she would produce sounds herself – banging doors, tapping things, shouting.

John (hypoauditory) always joins in Helen's 'noise making'. However, his hypersensitivity to smells prevents him coming too close to anybody and makes any activities in the kitchen intolerable.

Vicky is hypersensitive to sounds, touch and smell. If she is being touched by somebody, she immediately smells the place of touch, and more often than not she takes off her jacket or dress with this 'spoilt spot' and refuses to wear it again unless it is washed.

Hypersensitivity can also lead to two different experiences: disturbance by certain sensory stimuli and its opposite – fascination with certain stimuli. These experiences are very individual. The kinds of stimuli that are disturbing or fascinating vary from person to person. A sight/sound/smell that causes one child pain may be pleasurable to another.

All senses can be affected. Some people might find many noises and bright lights nearly impossible to bear; for others certain noises (children's voices, car horns, a kettle whistling) and the pitch of some sounds might cause a lot of discomfort. A woman with Asperger syndrome cannot tolerate somebody whistling. She describes it as a 'physical abuse' because whistling causes her body to tremble and even ache. Besides, not only certain sounds but also any sudden unpredictable sounds can be painful. The fear of noise that hurts the ears is often the cause of many bad behaviours and tantrums. Some autistic children, for instance, can break the telephone because they are afraid it will ring (Grandin 1996b).

Consider the following example given by Marc Fleisher, a person with Asperger syndrome, and try to imagine the 'perceptual world' of this student at the moment of 'ruler-danger'. No wonder, the possible challenging behaviours of the person would seem as 'coming out of the blue' and the ABC (Antecedent – Behaviour – Consequence) principles of Applied Behaviour Analysis (when we look for triggers of challenging behaviours) are useless in this case, as we should deal with 'probable future antecedent' triggering the behaviour at present.

> You are in a room with an autistic individual and you are trying to give a math lesson. On the table, and among other items, you have a wooden ruler. At one particular instant, you unintentionally brush your arm against the ruler so that it now is only just balancing on the table edge with almost half its length in the air with no support. Provided there is no draught the ruler will probably still remain, but shove it any more, and it certainly fall, making a loud clatter on the stone floor…
>
> …you probably would not even have been aware that you had moved the ruler. Many autistic people are very susceptible to noise. Suddenly their whole world is focusing on that ruler – all other objects in the room seem to dim. The ruler! The ruler! That's all that matters. If it falls it will make a loud clatter on the floor. (Fleisher 2001, pp.323–4)

Some autistic people often find it impossible to touch some objects. Donna Williams calls one of her particular texture problems 'wool on wool', i.e.

intolerance of hair rubbing against hair or cloth against cloth. It means that it is difficult to her to tolerate people's hair rubbing on her or their clothes rubbing her clothes, and it is hard to tolerate putting a woollen jumper over her head or walking on some carpets with certain types of socks (Williams 1996).

The most often reported visual sensitivities are sensitivity to bright light, fluorescent light, colours and certain patterns (especially stripes). The light sensitivity in autism coincides with the symptoms of Scotopic Sensitivity/Irlen Syndrome (SS/IS) identified by Helen Irlen (1991) (see Chapter 6). Many autistic people confirm that bright lights and sunshine disturb them and often cause distortions. For example, as a child, Nony (1993) found it difficult to walk in town on a sunny day. Her eyes would close and she would have to turn into a darker doorway or cover her eyes to get them open enough to see; the glare of sidewalks and shop windows was too much for her. Some people report that on bright days their sight blurs (White and White 1987).

Alex, an autistic boy, cannot tolerate contrasts: it is impossible for him to walk along the street in the dark with cars with bright lights passing by. Even his tinted (very dark) glasses do not help much.

Fluorescent light has been reported by many autistic individuals to be very difficult to tolerate, because they can see a 60-cycle flicker. Problems with flickering can range from excessive eyestrain to seeing a room pulsate on and off (Grandin 1996a). Some people report that they feel sleepy when the fluorescent lights are on.

Sensitivity to colours and colour contrast is another visual problem for some autistic people. For example, Liane Willey, a woman with Asperger syndrome, finds it difficult to look at pastels as they make her feel icky, queasy and uneven. They drown her (Willey 1999).

Some autistic individuals cannot tolerate food of some particular taste, smell, texture or appearance (certain colours, for example), or even the sound it produces when they chew it.

What to look for:

1. Squints or closes eyes in bright light

2. Gets easily frustrated/tired under fluorescent lights

3. Gets frustrated with certain colours

4. Gets frustrated with certain sounds

5. Tries to destroy/break objects producing sounds (clock, telephone, toy, etc.)

6. Cannot tolerate certain textures

7. Cannot tolerate some smells/tastes

8. Cannot tolerate certain movements/body postures

9. Fears falling or height

Fascination with certain stimuli is an opposite of disturbance by certain stimuli, caused also by hypersensitivity. These two features are like two sides of one and the same coin. The only difference is, while disturbance causes pain, fascination gives pleasant experiences and brings calm and peace to autistic people (although at the cost of their withdrawal).

Sometimes people with autism, when they have given up fighting in an incomprehensible world, rescue themselves from overload to an entertaining, secure and hypnotic level of hyper-: watching the reflection of every element of light and colour, tracing every patterned shape and vibration of noise as it bounces off the walls (Williams 1994). Donna Williams names it as the beautiful side of autism, sanctuary of the prison. Autistic people can be fascinated with different sensory stimuli, such as the smell of melting candles, rice cooking, the feel of velvet and marble, the taste of smooth, satiny wood, the pit-pat of bare feet on tiles, the look of clouds gliding high, the feel of a horse's nose, the chalky taste of seashells (O'Neill 1999).

The sources of fascinations are very individual. For example, to Liane Willey (1999) such visual elements as linear lines, symmetry, balance, straightness, perfect alignments, squares and triangles were appealing. Wendy Lawson (1998) finds certain colours fascinating. Her favourite colours are rich emerald green, royal blue, purple, and turquoise. A typical picture of an individual with autism is when he is sitting staring transfixed at the crystal, turning it around and around in front of his eyes, catching rainbows (Oliver in Williams 1994).

One and the same stimulus can cause disturbance and fascination to different children.

What to look for:

1. Is fascinated with coloured and shining objects

2. Is fascinated with certain sounds

3. Is fascinated with certain textures

4. Is fascinated with certain smells/tastes

5. Is often engaged in complex ritualistic body movements, especially when frustrated or bored

6. Spins, jumps, rocks, etc. especially when frustrated or bored

> *Vicky hates the sound of running water, whereas John is fascinated with it. Alex is disturbed by bright lights, whereas Helen enjoys looking at them.*

Inconsistency of perception (fluctuation)

One of the baffling features of autistic people is their inconsistent perception of sensory stimuli. Two types of this inconsistency can be distinguished: fluctuation between hyper- and hypo-; and fluctuation between hyper-/hypo- and normal ('in' and 'out').

Fluctuation between hyper- and hyposensitivity is quite common. A child who appears to be deaf on one occasion may react to an everyday sound on another occasion as if it is causing acute pain; visual stimuli that may appear so bright on one occasion will on another occasion appear very dim. Similarly, reaction to pain may vary from complete insensitivity to apparent 'over-reaction' to the slightest knock (Jordan and Powell 1990). Sometimes a particular food, which is one of the favourites, will be rejected for no particular reason (Legge 2002).

Ornitz and Ritvo (1968) suggest that autism is characterized by fluctuation between states of over- and underarousal resulting in a failure to modulate sensory intake adequately and an unstable perceptual experience. The authors argue that the individual's sensitivity to stimuli fluctuates and depends on whether the person is in a state of over- or underarousal. Ornitz (1989) states that the disturbance of sensory modulation involves all sensory modalities and is manifested as both under- and overreactivity to sensory stimuli and as self-stimulation. Ornitz suggests that optimal levels of stimulation will vary across autistic persons as a function of developmental level, degree of familiarity with the situation, and biologically based individual differences, including the severity of autistic disorder. This model assumes that the disturbances of sensory modulation are the primary symptoms and the impairments of social interaction, communication, language and bizarre behaviour are consequences of a dysmodulation of sensory input.

In personal accounts people with autism describe their experience of 'unreliable' perception, for example:

> Sometimes when other kids spoke to me I would scarcely hear, then sometimes they sounded like bullets. (White and White 1987)

> It [hearing] gets louder sometimes... Things seem suddenly closer sometimes. Sometimes things get suddenly brighter. (Oliver in Williams 1994, p.189)

Fluctuation between hyper-/hypo- and normal ('in' and 'out'). Dr Freeman (1993, p.5) describes perception of the world by people with autism 'like an FM radio that is not exactly tuned on the station when you are driving down the freeway. Sometimes the world comes in clearly and at other times it does not.'

People with autism contribute to the explanation of this phenomenon. Donna Williams (1994) compares autism with a seesaw: when it is up or down she cannot see a whole life; when it is passing through in the middle she gets to see a glimpse of the life she would have if she were not autistic. J.G.T. VanDalen terms it as 'suddenly falling out of autism' and describes his personal experience of this process as follows: 'the stay in the non-autistic condition lasts only a few minutes...the exit-procedure occurs instantaneously, the return is gradual' (1995, pp.13, 14).

Interestingly, it is these experiences that have brought VanDalen to the conclusions that:

- Autism is primarily a perceptual deficit, as during these short periods when his 'perception was normalized' he 'noticed above all the diffused fear (he constantly experienced) was completely vanished...the habitual occupation with inanimate physical objects disappeared in favour of all the (warm) feelings that belonged to normal relationships' (p.13).

- 'The degree of autism within an individual can vary considerably even to the point of 'suddenly falling out of it' (p.13).

What to look for:

1. Responds differently (pleasure – indifference – distress) to the same visual/auditory/olfactory/gustatory/tactile stimuli, movement activities (swings, slides, spinning, etc.)

2. May have different muscle tone (low – high)

3. Pencil lines, letters, words, etc. are uneven (e.g. sometimes too tight, sometimes too faint)

Vicky can eat everything she is given one day, and refuses to eat even her favourite food (sausage) on the other. Alex can respond differently to the same visual (colours, patterns) or auditory stimuli (the sound of heating system, fan) depending on his physical state and the value of his 'cup'.

(See Vulnerability to sensory overload below.)

Fragmented perception (perception 'in bits', stimulus overselectivity)

Because of gestalt perception, when too much information needs to be processed simultaneously, very often people with autism are not able to 'break' the whole picture into meaningful units and to interpret objects, people and surroundings as constituents of a whole situation. Instead they process 'bits' that happen to get their attention.

This fragmented perception can affect all the senses:

> I had always known that the world was fragmented. My mother was a smell and a texture, my father was a tone, and my older brother was something, which was moving about. (Williams 1992, p.11)

> I remember being attracted to pieces of people's faces. I might have liked the color of the eyes, the texture of the hair or the straightness of the teeth. (Willey 1999, p.23)

> Sometimes people would have to repeat a particular sentence several times for me as I would hear it in bits and the way in which my mind had segmented their sentence into words left me with a strange and sometimes unintelligible message. It was a bit like when someone plays around with the volume switch on TV. (Williams 1992, p.61)

The perception of parts instead of wholes and utilizing only a very limited amount of available information is known as stimulus overselectivity (Lovaas *et al.* 1971). The result is that autistic people often react upon parts of objects or people as being complete entities:

> Where someone else may have seen 'crowd', I saw arm, person, mouth, face, hand, seat, person, eye… I was seeing ten thousand pictures to someone else's one. (Williams 1998, p.21)

> I did not see whole. I saw hair, I saw eyes, nose, mouth, chin, …not face. (Alex in Williams 1999, p.180)

One of the theories attempting to explain this phenomenon is the central coherence theory (Frith 1989; Happe 1994): people with autism lack the 'built-in form of coherence' and, as a result, they see the world as less integrated, i.e. analytically rather than holistically.

In contrast to weak central coherence hypothesis in autism, one may hypothesize that people with autism possess a very strong drive for coherence (i.e. holistic perception of the world) with the main difficulty being to break the gestalt into meaningful units in order to analyse them separately. Without perceiving separate units as integrated parts of a whole, it is impossible to interpret the situation. Brad Rand, a person with autism, suggests that one of possible causes for seeing things as disconnected might be lacking the resource(s) to process all relevant parts of a stimulus at once. This, in turn, could result in either overly narrow attentional focus or insufficient memory resources to handle the task. In this case, the relatedness of things disappears. Everything seems to be conceptually a separate and unrelated entity; 'on' and 'next' and 'in front of' do not mean much anymore, because whatever something is 'on', 'next to' or 'in front of' no longer has a reality until it itself is focused upon directly (Williams 1999).

Fragmented perception caused by inability to 'break gestalt' into integrated and meaningful parts fits into the definition of weak central coherence. Thus, we may conclude that weak central coherence theory may be applied at later stages of sensory perceptual processing.

The perception 'in bits' can be clearly seen in drawings by some autistic children. A 13-year-old verbal autistic boy was drawing a church (Figure 3.3). He was commenting while drawing: 'I'm going to draw a church. A flag on the church. A clock – twenty past two. And then I'm going to draw a big window at the church. A bell – goes ding-ding. Done it!'

Figure 3.3 'Church'. Drawing by D., 13 years old

In the state of fragmented perception, the person has great difficulty in dealing with people as they seem not only to consist of many unconnected pieces but also the movements of these 'bits of people' are unpredictable. The strategy to cope with the problem is to avoid people and never look at them. It does not mean that they cannot *see* an entire person (perceptual level). They seem to be unable to *process* the meaning of an entire person but process them bit by bit instead. As a result the mental image of a 'collection of bits' is often meaningless and often frightening. Fragmentation complicates the interpretation of facial expressions and body language and thus hinders or even blocks the development of non-verbal communication.

Let us have a look at the children's drawings again. Two autistic boys drew 'portraits' of their mothers (Figures 3.4 and 3.5). It is no wonder that these children find social interaction very difficult, if not impossible. We often describe them as 'aliens', but don't we look aliens to them?

Figure 3.4 'Mother's portrait', by D.

Figure 3.5 'Mother's portrait', by Alex

This category also includes a sort of 'tunnel vision' experienced by some people with autism:

> I picked up his hand and looked at it closely. I traced it with my eyes from the fingers to the shoulder, from the shoulder to the eyes, down to the nose and mouth. Ian was a jigsaw of bits that my mind was in no state to make sense of as a whole. (Williams 1999, p.21)

Fragmentation may be felt in all sensory modalities. For example, Alex is sure that he (like everybody else) has two foreheads and always asks his mother to kiss 'both' – 'this one and that one'.

As some individuals with autism perceive everything in pieces they need time to adjust to different surroundings. As the number of objects seen by them is greater (because they see different images of one and the same object from different angles – VanDalen 1995) – they do not feel safe in this chaos of things and people. As a consequence of this fragmented perception autistic individuals exhibit maintenance of sameness, resistance to change, anxiety in unfamiliar places.

Perception 'in bits' means that autistic individuals define people and places and things by these bits. They can suddenly find once familiar things to be strikingly unfamiliar if slight components are changed, such as when the furniture has been moved or someone does not wear the same coat as usual (Williams 1996). As they process what they perceive piece by piece and not as a whole, they recognize things and people by the 'sensory pieces' they store as their definitions. For instance, they may 'recognize' their mother by the colour of her dress and may not 'recognize' her if she wears a dress of different colour, or they may know people and objects by smell, sound, intonation, the way they move, etc.

People with Asperger syndrome (especially women) are reported to have a very poor sense of direction. When they approach even a familiar street from an unusual direction, they do not immediately recognize it.

Another 'side-effect' of perception in bits is 'a sense of fear that is not specifically related to certain objects but is originated in the fact that [the] first encounter with a physical object is a partial one' (VanDalen 1995, p.12). VanDalen compares this experience with a confrontation with a silhouette in the dark: one knows that something is there but it is not altogether immediately clear what it is.

It is difficult to identify the 'sensory concepts' the child has stored in his memory. However, some parents intuitively 'know' what might upset their child.

What to look for:

1. Resists any change

2. Selects for attention minor aspects of objects in the environment instead of the whole scene

3. Gets lost easily

4. Does not recognize people in unfamiliar clothes, on photographs

5.   Hears a few words instead of the whole sentence

6.   Complains about some parts of the clothes, smells of some pieces of food, etc.

7.   Is confused with the food he used to like

8.   Complains about limbs, part of the body

9.   Resists new motor activities

Vicky often has problems with parts of her clothes – 'It hurts here' (trying to tear off her right sleeve while feeling comfortable with her left one).

Alex 'sees in bits': 'Her leg disturbs me'. 'Dasha's [the cat] head has turned round.'

Distorted perception

Although fragmented perception can be also termed distorted, in this book distorted perception means not fragmentation but rather change (distortion) in the perception of the form, space, sound, etc. Distortions are reported to become worse in the state of nervous overarousal and information overload.

In the field of vision the most common distortions reported by the individuals with autism are poor/distorted depth and space perception, seeing a 2D world, 'double vision', distortions of shape, size and movement. Because of these distortions, their perception of space may be different; space may seem to be expanded, or, on the contrary, look smaller.

Problems with proprioceptors may bring trouble with understanding boundaries and relationships between objects in space and their own bodies; sometimes they are confused about the parts of their bodies. For example, Oliver (in Williams 1994, p.191) describes his experiences of 'losing his legs': 'I had no sense of my body from my waist down. I feel like I was flying.' As a teenager, Donna Williams spent many hours trying to shake a hand off an arm without the perception that both were part of her body (1996, p.14). Some people experience difficulties in perception of movement:

> Occasionally I lost all sense of perspective. Something would seem monstrously large if coming towards me at speed, or if I was unprepared. Someone suddenly leaning over me could frighten me enormously. I felt something was falling onto me and that I'd be crushed underneath it. (Gerland 1997)

> The bitumen floor of the school playground intrigued me and I noticed that as I ran it seemed to run with me. (Lawson 1998, p.29)

One of the characteristic behaviours of autistic children is to spin themselves and enjoy swings without becoming dizzy. The individuals with autism report that these activities help them normalize perception and a vestibular system. Many autistic children would climb to great heights and jump down in desperate attempt (though not consciously) to normalize a vestibular system.

Russell (1994) suggests that one of the basic deficits in autism might be disturbance at the stage of 'efferent copying'. In normal development the 'efferent copying' gives the sense of one's own agency, i.e. the nervous system does not only control movements of the head and eyes to scan the environment or keep track of moving objects, but also records those movements in order to distinguish the case where the movement is in the person's head and eyes, and the world is still. In autism, the researcher suggests, the disturbance at the stage of 'efferent copying' prevents the person having a sense of himself or herself as an agent. In this case the person would not get dizzy in the normal way from spinning and, moreover, might seek for the kinds of sensations that would give movement stimulation free from recording head and eye movements in relation to the world.

What to look for:

1. Fears heights, stairs, escalators

2. Has difficulty catching balls

3. Appears startled when being approached

4. Compulsive repetitive hand, head or body movements that fluctuate between near and far

5. Pronunciation problems

6. Unable to distinguish between some sounds

7. Hits eyes/ears/nose/oneself

8. Difficulty with hopping, jumping, skipping, riding a tricycle/bicycle

9. Climbs high into a tree, jumps off tall fences, etc.

Helen does not seem to feel boundaries of her body and its position in the classroom. She often hits herself when confused with the instruction to move her body, for example, 'Don't lean over the table.'

Vicky has poor depth and space perception. She is afraid of descending the stairs, and when ascending she lifts her feet too high above the stairs.

Sensory agnosia (difficulty interpreting a sense)

The consequence of being unable to filter sensory information and being flooded with sensory stimuli at the rate the person cannot cope, is being able to sense (see, hear, etc.), but unable to attach the meaning to (i.e. to interpret) the sensations. The person is 'blind while seeing' (VanDalen 1995), 'deaf while hearing', etc. Donna Williams (1994; 1996; 1998; 1999) calls these experiences 'meaning-blind/meaning-deaf/touch-dead'. She compares this condition with being deaf-blind, the main difference being, the blind get meaning without seeing, while the meaning-blind see without meaning. The deaf-blind may have lost their sense but the meaning-blind/deaf lost the sense (meaning) (Williams 1994; 1998).

In the state of sensory agnosia, interpretation of any sense can be lost; they often act as if they were really blind, deaf, numb, sometimes 'dead'. It is a very frightening experience. Each individual develops his/her own strategies to cope with it.

What to look for:

1. Feels/acts blind/deaf/etc.

2. Rituals

3. Has difficulty in interpreting smells/tastes

4. Seems not to know what their body is doing

5. Becomes disoriented after a change in head position

> *Helen often behaves as if she were deaf; she does not react to any sound at all and does not seem to understand what she is expected to do.*

Delayed perception (delayed processing)

It is not uncommon for autistic children to exhibit delayed responses to stimuli:

> As a child…it appeared as though I didn't feel pain or discomfort, didn't want help, didn't know what I was saying, didn't listen or didn't watch. By the time some of these sensations, responses or comprehensions were decoded and processed for meaning and personal significance, and I'd accessed the means of responding, I was fifteen minutes, one day, a week, a month, even a year away from the context in which the experiences happened. (Williams 1996, p.90)

A person can be delayed on every sensory channel.

Concerning vision, VanDalen (1995) attempts to give one of the possible explanations of this phenomenon: the acquisition of the full meaning requires some observation time from different points of view; besides, people with autism must translate perceptual configurations into their proper terminology.

Perception by parts requires a great amount of time and effort to interpret the whole. Many autistic individuals emphasize the amount of 'thinking' necessary to make sense of the world. VanDalen describes the process as 'thinking in the background' – constructing an object by using explicit trains of thought, whereas for non-autistic people this process is automatic and effortless. To illustrate the point VanDalen describes how he perceives objects:

> When I am confronted with a hammer, I am initially not confronted with a hammer at all but solely with a number of unrelated parts: I notify a cubical piece of iron within its neighborhood a coincidental bar-like piece of wood. After that, I am struck by the coincidental nature of the iron and the wooden thing resulting in the unifying perception of a hammerlike configuration. The name 'hammer' is not immediately within reach but appears when the configuration has been sufficiently stabilized over time. Finally, the use of a tool becomes clear when I realize that this perceptual configuration, known as 'hammer', can be used to do carpenter's work. (VanDalen 1995, p.11)

The experience of 'delayed hearing' is termed by Dr Rimland 'delayed mental audition': when the question has been sensed and recorded without interpretation until the second (internalized) hearing. Rimland describes the effect of 'delayed mental audition' as an echo; and the sound of the echo-like voice is high-pitched, hollow and parrot-like, i.e. the internally experienced voice duplicates precisely the classical manner of speech of an autistic child. Rimland names it the 'closed loop' phenomenon when the stimuli enter memory and later emerge unchanged (Rimland 1964, pp.178–9).

In the most extreme cases, it can take years to process what has been said. Sometimes it takes days, weeks or months. The words, phrases, sentences, sometimes the whole situations, are stored and they can be triggered at anytime. In less extreme cases, to process something takes seconds or minutes. They may be able to repeat back what has been said without comprehension that will come later.

Due to delayed processing autistic individuals may need some time to process the question and their response. (Immediate responses are often given on 'autopilot', triggered by memories.) Before proper response autistic people must go through a number of separate stages in perception, and if this long decision-chain is interrupted by the outside world, the autistic person must start all over again because overselectivity has changed the scene completely (VanDalen 1995). In other words, an interruption effectively wipes away any intermediate result, confronting the autistic person literally 'for the first time' with the same object/event/situation. VanDalen suggests that autism could possibly be understood as an extension of the processing time of impressions. This definition implies the importance of giving autistic people time to enable them to finish their perceptual work successfully and 'to experience meaning that is awaiting on the end of the long road of perception' (VanDalen 1995).

All these 'continuous obligatory thinking activities connected with everyday object-perception' (VanDalen) require much effort and energy, that is another reason for autistic children to resist any changes, and to prefer familiar surroundings where it is much easier for them to control their perceptual world. Every step of perception they experience explicitly, in a non-automatic way with a great mental effort involved. That is why they are often unable to start the action immediately.

There are several consequences of delayed processing. One of them is 'experiencing meaning' out of the context it should have been experienced, i.e. new experiences, no matter how similar to previous ones, are perceived as new, unfamiliar and unpredictable, and responses to them are poor regardless of the number of times the person has experienced the same thing. Another one is that, as the amount of time needed to process any experience often remains slow (or delayed), regardless of having had similar experiences in the past, things do not get easier with time or learning (Williams 1996). They are not able to generalize and apply something they have learned in one situation to another.

Their subjective experience of time is also different from that of non-autistics. For them, time might seem faster, whereas non-autistic people may think that autistic children are slow in their decision-making.

What to look for:

1.   Response to visual/auditory/gustatory/olfactory/tactile stimuli is delayed

2.   Echolalia in monotonous, high-pitched, parrot-like voice

3.   Any experiences are perceived as new and unfamiliar, regardless of the number of times the person has experienced the same thing

4.   Very poor at sports

5.   Seems oblivious to risks of heights, etc.

6.   Holds head upright, even when leaning or bending over

> *All the children in the class display delayed perception to the auditory stimuli; John, Helen and Vicky could respond to the question in a few minutes; Alex sometimes gives responses even in a few days. It is very difficult to connect his 'announcements' with the question he was asked a few days before. To an outsider, these responses, unconnected to the present situation, seem weird.*

Vulnerability to sensory overload

Many autistic people are very vulnerable to sensory overload. They may become overloaded in situations that would not bother other people (Blackburn 1997; Lawson 1998; Morris 1999; Willey 1999). The causes of information of overload can be:

- the inability to filter out irrelevant or excessive information

- delayed processing

- if the person works in mono but is forced to attend to the information from several channels

- distorted or fragmented perception, resulting in anxiety, confusion, frustration and stress that, in turn, may lead to hypersensitivity.

Donna Williams (1996) emphasizes that sensory hypersensitivity can happen both independently of information overload and as a direct result of it. The overload can lead to hypersensitivity (with its resulting physical pain, tantrums and difficult behaviour). Sometimes it can result in 'accumulation of unknown knowing', i.e. when information gets processed outside of conscious awareness so that one is not aware of what one knows nor able consciously or voluntarily to access that knowledge, though sometimes it can be triggered or cued by something outside (Williams 1996); or might go further to 'total systems shutdowns' (Blackburn 1997; Williams 1996). The process from hypersensitivity to systems shutdowns may be fast (i.e. sensory discomfort may be short lasting or not experienced at all) or may be slow (i.e. sensory discomfort may be prolonged).

The information overload may be dispersed before it leads to systems shutdowns or it may not. In the first case, a person may experience severe sensory hypersensitivity (colours becoming too intense, light becoming too bright, certain pitches becoming intolerable, certain patterns becoming obtrusively distinct, touch may feel 'prickly' or 'ticklish', or provoke 'shock') yet continue to process information. If information overload is not diffused in time, it can result in temporal sensory agnosia – a temporary inability to process touch, sound or visual information (Williams 1996). For example:

> Overload had set in. Explanations were just blah-blah-blah... My vision started to climb... The lights became brighter. I was tickled by the effect on my senses and began to giggle. The hypersensitivity...climbed even higher...I squinted and grinned, the strain and the confusion of the sudden change from happy to excited to tortured took place within the space of fifteen minutes with no cues to tell me why or what I was feeling and no time to reflect. My ship was sinking and no one knew. (Williams 1994, p.106)

> Together, the sharp sounds and the bright lights were more than enough to overload my senses. My head would feel tight, my stomach would churn, and my pulse would run my heart ragged until I found a safety zone. (Willey 1999, p.22)

The causes of information overload on auditory level are reported not to do with the perception of pitch and volume but rather with the number of simultaneous sound sources, the duration of these stimuli and the rate of the bombardment relative to process capacity. Then hearing becomes acute, sounds that are normally inaudible can be as audible as usual sounds, the perception of these additional sounds can make them intensely unbearable (Williams 1996). Donna Williams considers this reverberation of sound as one of the biggest contributors to sound information overload.

The visual equivalent of sound reverberation, according to Donna Williams, is light refraction (or 'shine') that can cause a visual effect of shooting out streams or 'sparks' of light and 'visually cutting up' people and objects. The same can happen with touch: when too much of visual and auditory information has been taken in, the sense of touch can be oversensitive, 'sharp as a pin', and to be touched can be 'shocking' (Williams 1996).

The threshold for processing sensory stimuli varies among autistic persons, at different ages and in different environments. For example:

> When I was a small child, my threshold for processing blah-blah was only a few seconds. When I was about ten or so, my threshold...was about five to ten minutes. When I was a teenager and up to my twenties, this threshold was about fifteen minutes to half an hour. Now it is about twenty to forty-five minutes. In a more accommodating environment...these thresholds could have been much higher than they were. (Williams 1996, p.204)

Dena Gitlitz (cited in Donnelly 1999) names it Eight Ball Theory: Eight Ball is similar to a juggler that can successfully juggle seven pins or balls but if you throw in one more they will drop them all. Dena has a limited capacity for 'how many balls she can juggle' successfully. This phenomenon could be called the 'rule of the last drop': if the child's inner 'cup' is full already (whatever the reasons for this may be) the slightest trigger (which on the days when the 'cup' is empty would not be noticed by the child) might produce an overload.

Each individual may cope with overwhelming stimuli in different ways: mono-processing, avoidance of direct perception, withdrawal, stereotypies.

What to look for:

1. Sudden outbursts of self-abuse/tantrums/difficult behaviours

2. Withdrawal

3. Tires very easily, especially when in noisy/bright places, or when standing

4.   Gets nauseated or vomits from excessive movements (swings, merry-go-rounds, cars, etc.)

Alex is very vulnerable to sensory overload. The speed with which his 'cup has been filled' depends on the number and intensity of the stimuli. For example, if there are two or more people talking at once, he is sure to be overwhelmed; bright lights (especially fluorescent lights) and lots of movement around him will cause his outburst in a few minutes.

Note

1.   Gestalt is a shape, pattern, or structure, which as an object of perception forms a specific whole and has properties, which cannot be completely deduced from a knowledge of the properties of its parts. The term was originally used by a 'school' of psychology – Gestalt psychology, which emphasizes the relational aspects, especially of perceiving, in strong opposition to atomistic concepts.

Chapter 4

Perceptual Styles

Autistic children seem to develop (voluntarily or involuntarily) the ability to control their awareness of incoming sensory stimuli in order to survive in a world bombarding them with extraneous information. These compensatory or defensive strategies are reflected in acquired perceptual styles.

Most commonly reported perceptual styles are:

- mono-processing
- peripheral perception (avoidance of direct perception)
- systems shutdowns
- compensating for unreliable sense by other senses
- resonance
- daydreaming.

Mono-processing

To avoid overload of sensory information, only one modality is processed consciously by the brain (though subconsciously a great amount of information may get in – 'accumulation of unknown knowing' – Williams 1994). The person might focus on one sense, for example, sight, and might see every minute detail of the object. However, while his vision is on, the person might lose awareness of any information coming through other senses. Thus, while the person sees something, he does not hear anything, and does not feel touch, etc. When the visual stimulus fades out, the sound could be processed, but then the sound is the only information the person is dealing with (i.e. disconnected from sight). As the person focuses on only one modality at a time, the sound may be experienced louder because it is all the person focuses on (hypersensitivity).

According to the number of senses working at a time the person can be classified into 'multi-track' versus mono-processing (Williams 1996) or 'being singly channelled' (Lawson 1999). The ability to receive and process information via multiple sources can also be referred to as 'polytropism', in contrast to 'monotropism' (using one channel at a time) (Lawson 2001; Murray 1992).

Wendy Lawson believes that central coherence (the ability to draw connections together from the 'big picture') can only occur with least effort, when one has access to the big picture via many different channels (polytropism). Wendy argues that in monotropism, where all the attention is gathered into one place, there is an extreme central coherence but of different type. 'Monotropic central coherence' excludes information from outside the attention channel (Lawson 2001).

Most people use their senses simultaneously. When they are hearing something, they are still aware of what they see and feel emotionally and physically, because they are 'multi-tracked'. For people who work in mono to process the meaning of what they are listening to while being touched may be to have no idea where they were being touched or what they thought or felt about it. To process the location or special significance of being touched while someone is showing them something means that they see nothing but meaningless colour and form and movement (Williams 1996). For example, Donna Williams's inner-body sense, like everything else, was mostly in mono: if she touched her leg she would feel it on her hand or on her leg but not both at the same time (Williams 1994). She had big restrictions in being able to process information from the outside and inside at the same time, for example, touching the furniture she could feel the texture of the wood but would have no sense of her own hand. She could also switch channels and feel her own hand but would lose sensation of what her hand was in contact with. Without being able to process her own body sensations in relations to textures it was, perceptually, as though either she did not exist and other things did or she existed and they did not. She was either in a constant state of jolting perceptual shifts or remained on one sensory channel or the other (Williams 1998).

Actually, this type of processing is taken advantage of by the parents of some autistic children who are 'picky eaters'. Children with very restricted diets (hypersensitive to taste/smell, texture of the food) will eat better if they are watching a video, listening to music or talking to someone.

Jared Blackburn (1999) describes the trouble he had processing many things at once. For example, he could not take notes at the lecture because he could either listen or write, but not both. Many of his teachers thought he was being lazy or inattentive because he did not take notes and did not look at them and had a blank look on his face, but he was actually almost hypnotically focused on what they were saying. It is a matter of taking one thing at a time (Kathy French cited in Donnelly 1999).

Individuals with autism define this mono-processing (monotropism) as one of their involuntary adaptations to avoid sensory overload or hypersensitivity:

> If I'm looking at something and listening to something at the same time, too much information might come in my eyes and ears at the same time, so I might touch something. That gets information going in a different sense, through my touch, and it lets my eyes and ears have a rest. (Rand, undated)

It is a mechanism by which the time and energy that goes into processing gets spread a little less thinly than it otherwise might: switching between different channels gives them an opportunity to keep the remaining ones going more efficiently (Williams 1996; 1998). Donna Williams illustrates this phenomenon as follows:

> This is like having one employee working in a huge department store instead of having a whole staff. If a customer has a demand in the shoe department whilst the worker is presently dealing with a demand in the toy department, the customer in the shoe department wouldn't find anybody there...and sometimes (this single worker closes) the shop in different departments when she can't cope with the demand. (Williams 1996, pp.99, 100)

We should be aware of this style of perception in order to give the child information in a way he will be able to process. The matter is complicated by the fact, that they could switch channels and our task is to find out which channel 'is open' to get the information.

What to look for:

1. Does not seem to see if listening/smelling/feeling taste/touching, etc.

2. Does not seem to hear if looking/smelling/feeling taste/touching, etc.

3. Does not seem to feel taste if looking/listening/smelling/touching, etc.

4. Does not seem to smell if seeing/hearing, etc.

5. Does not seem to feel being touched if looking/listening, etc.

6. Fails to define the texture or location of touch

7. Does not seem to know the position of the body in space/what the body is doing when looking at/listening to something

8. Does not seem to mind any movements when looking at/listening to something

> *The teacher shows a card with number ten. John is looking at it very attentively but he 'loses' the auditory instruction, 'Say the previous number', and seems very confused without any understanding of what is expected of him.*

Peripheral perception (avoidance of direct perception)

One of the characteristics of autism is avoidance of eye contact. It is an example of peripheral perception, as it turns out that avoidance of direct perception is not restricted only to vision but also includes other sensory systems.

One of the theories to account for this is that people with autism use peripheral vision because their central vision is hypo- while their peripheral vision is hyper-. However, analysis of the personal accounts of individuals with autism shows that often they do not use their direct/central perception because 'it hurts', i.e. it is hyper-. For instance, for Nony eye contact was painful: 'It was not quite like a broken bone or a burn but it can only be described as pain' (Nony 1993).

Jean-Paul Bovee describes eye contact as something that he always has trouble with, as all of the stress that is put on doing it makes him more nervous, tense, and scared. Jasmine O'Neill reports that 'gazing directly at people or animals is many times too overwhelming... Some autistic people don't even look at the eyes of actors or news reporters on television' (O'Neill 1999, p.26).

Some of the problems autistic people have with making eye contact may be nothing more than intolerance for the movement of the other person's eyes. Temple Grandin writes about an autistic person for whom looking at other people's eyes was difficult because the eyes did not stay still (Grandin 1996a).

Direct perception in autism is often hyper. It can cause sensory overload resulting in switching to mono:

> I actually hear you better when I am not looking at you...eye contact is...uncomfortable...[people] will never understand the battle I have gone through to be able to do this. (Lawson 1998, p.11)

Perceiving sound, visual stimuli, etc. directly and consciously may often result in fragmentation: the person can interpret the part but lose the whole, and incoming information is interpreted piece by piece. Donna Williams (1998) explains that when taking things indirectly, peripherally, the fragmentation did not happen; things were more cohesive, they retained context, whereas the mind-jolting senses of direct vision and direct hearing could not be consistently relied upon as meaningful primary senses.

Some autistic people seem to be hypersensitive when they are approached directly by other people:

> Dr Marek was 'touching' me with his eyes... I was afraid... I was being hurt. (Williams 1994, p.121)

> It can feel creepy to be searched with the eyes. (O'Neill 1999, p.26)

> Someone looking directly into my eyes felt like an attack. (Nony 1993)

> When I look someone straight in the eye, particularly someone I am
> not familiar with...I feel as if their eyes are burning me and I really
> feel as if I am looking into the face of an alien. (Jackson 2002, pp.70,
> 71)

For some, if they are looked at directly (even if they do not 'return the gaze'), they may feel it as 'a touch' – sort of 'distance touching' with actual tactile experience that can be painful. Avoidance of direct perception for autistic people is another involuntary adaptation that helps them to survive in a sensory distorted world by avoiding (or decreasing) information overload.

Autistic children often seem to look past things and are completely 'absent' from the scene. However, it could be their attempt to avoid experiencing a visual/auditory stimulus directly. This strategy gives them the ability to take in sensory information with meaning.

They can often understand things better by attending to them indirectly, for example, by looking or listening peripherally (such as out of the corner of one's eye or by looking at or listening to something else). In this case it is a kind of indirectly confrontational approach in contrast to the 'normal' directly confrontational one (Williams 1998). The same is true for other senses if they are hypersensitive: indirect perception of smell or 'instrumental touch' (Williams 1994) are often defensive mechanisms to avoid overload.

What to look for:

1. Avoids direct eye contact

2. Reacts to the instructions better when they are 'addressed to the wall'

3. Can tolerate only 'instrumental' (not 'social') touch

4. Avoids direct smell/taste

5. A very careful eater

6. Has difficulty in imitating/copying movements

7. Avoids balancing activities

Alex, John and Vicky 'hear better' (i.e. react to the instructions) if the instructions are 'addressed to the wall'. Alex and Helen often use their peripheral vision and seem to see what is going on without directly looking at it. Alex cannot tolerate it when someone is looking at him directly and makes them turn away ('Don't look!' 'Turn away!'). He even complains if the cat is looking at him.

Systems shutdowns

Too much sensory overload may result in systems shutdowns, in which the person loses some or all of the normal functioning. Shutdown may feel different to different people, but is extremely unpleasant (Blackburn 1997).

When the person cannot cope with sensory information, he may shut down some or all sensory channels. Many autistic children are suspected to be deaf, as they sometimes do not react to sounds. Their hearing, however, is often even more acute than average, but they learn to 'switch it off' when they experience information overload. A child with sensory overload learns to avoid overwhelming sensory bombardment early in life. When sensory input becomes too intense and often painful a child learns to shut off his sensory channels and withdraw into his own world. Temple Grandin (1996b; 2000) hypothesizes that by doing this the autistic child creates his or her own self-imposed sensory deprivation that leads to secondary central nervous system (CNS) abnormalities that happen as a result of the autistic child's avoidance of input. To back up her argument Grandin (1996b) cited animal and human studies that show that restriction of sensory input causes the CNS to become overly sensitive to stimulation (Aftanas and Zubeck 1964; Melzack and Burns 1965; Simon and Land 1987). The effects of early sensory restriction are often long lasting. The brain waves of autistic children also show signs of high arousal (Hutt *et al.* 1964). The hypersensitivity caused by sensory deprivation seems to be relatively permanent. Autopsy studies indicate that cerebellar abnormalities occur before birth (Bauman 1991). However, the limbic system, which also has abnormalities, is not mature until the child is two years old. Temple Grandin argues that the possibility of secondary damage of the nervous system may explain why young children receiving early intervention have a better prognosis than children who do not receive special treatment do.

The research on primates has shown that early social isolation may result in deficiencies in social behaviours among primates ('primate isolation syndrome'). Isolation early in life results in significant changes in early experiences. These differences in experience may result in central nervous system modifications related to social deprivation. 'By the time significant psychopathological systems demand intervention later in life, some aspects of the disorder may be attributable to the primary process, but others may reflect behavioural and neurobiological aspects of the primate isolation syndrome' (Kraemer 1985, p.154). This argument was put forward by Kraemer in the context of schizophrenia. However, it could be applied to autism as well.

Systems shutdowns may be considered as an involuntary adaptation (compensation) when the brain shuts certain systems off to improve the level of functioning in others (Williams 1996). Donna Williams distinguishes three basic forms of systems shutdowns:

1.   Shutdown in the ability to simultaneously process sensory information and thought, feeling, body sensation or the monitoring of intentional and voluntary expression: all processing capacity may be diverted to processing incoming sensory information and no connections may be made to responding to that information. Donna Williams calls this state 'all other, no self'. For example, Temple Grandin (1996a) remembers how at the age of three she was frustrated because although she could understand what people said to her, she could not get her words out. On the other hand, incoming information, which has previously been processed, may be responded to at the expense of being able to further process any more information ('all self, no other').

2.   Shutdown in the ability to simultaneously process sensory information on several channels at once: Donna Williams subdivides it into temporary partial and extended systems shutdowns. Temporary systems shutdowns work by shutting down the ability to process information on a number of channels so that information can be efficiently processed on

whatever channel or channels are remaining. Temporary systems shutdowns can affect the processing of body awareness, touch, taste, smell, vision or hearing. They can be partial or almost total for any one sense. Partial shutdown means that only a part of processing may fall out of a particular sense (partial meaning deafness, partial meaning blindness, partial touch deadness, etc.). For example, a high-functioning person with autism could work with overload and shutdown in a way that never left him with any one system shutdown permanently but his systems in a constant state of shift (Jim in Williams 1994). Total shutdowns mean that though, for instance, eyes continue to see and ears to hear, the brain does not process any meaning of what is being seen or heard. Temple Grandin (1996a) calls these states visual/auditory tuneouts or whiteouts. Extended systems shutdowns are where a particular systems shutdown is a compensation to handle information overload over an extended amount of time: days, weeks and, very occasionally, a few months and even years.

3. Temporary or extended shutdown in the ability to maintain conscious and voluntary processing leads to the accumulation of the 'unknown knowing', i.e. the information is being perceived unconsciously, without the person's awareness of receiving it.

What to look for:

1. Appears to be a mindless follower

2. Surprises with knowing 'unknown' information

3. Sometimes does not react to any tactile stimuli/sounds/smells/tastes

4. Seems not to know how to move his body (unable to change body position to accommodate task)

5.   Becomes disoriented in noisy/bright places

6.   Rocks unconsciously during other activities (e.g. watching a video)

> *There are times when John and Helen seem to be mindless followers*
> *without any awareness of what is going on around them.*

Compensating for unreliable sense by other senses

Because of hypersensitivity, fragmented, distorted perception, delayed processing or sensory agnosia, one sense is never enough for autistic people to make sense of their environment. Thus, in the case of visual distortions and meaning-blindness, they use their ears, nose, tongue or hand to 'see', i.e. they compensate their temporary 'blindness' through other senses. For example, a child can tap objects to produce the sound in order to recognize what it is, because visual recognition can be fragmented and meaningless. Some children smell people and objects to identify them. To many autistic people the senses of touch and smell are reported to be more reliable. Many autistic children touch and smell things, some constantly tap everything to figure out where the boundaries are in their environment, like a blind person tapping with a cane. Their eyes and ears function, but they are not able to process incoming visual and auditory information (Grandin 1996a). Those who experience visual and auditory distortions prefer using touch to learn about their environment – they 'see' the world mostly through their fingers.

What to look for:

Tests visual/auditory/gustatory/olfactory/tactile information by other senses:

1.   Smells, licks, touches, or taps objects

2.   Looks for the source of the sound

3.   Inspects food before eating

4.   Watches their feet while walking

5.   Watches their hands while doing something

6.   Avoids climbing, jumping, walking on uneven ground

John and Alex smell, touch or tap objects to check their visual perception of them. Vicky always inspects her food (smells it) before eating it.

Resonance

Fascination with certain stimuli may culminate with 'losing oneself' in these stimuli to the extent that one can become 'resonant' with them. These terms were introduced by Donna Williams (1994; 1996; 1998; 1999) to define a state when one 'loses oneself in'/'becomes resonant' with something else. Here they are used to denote the higher degrees of fascination with sensory stimuli. The person can merge with (lose oneself in) different sensory stimuli as if the person became a part of the stimulus itself. These are very real experiences.

Wendy Lawson describes her experience when the colours and fragrance were so vibrant to her senses that she could 'feel' them. While watching some shiny things she felt a sense of connection, she felt safe, as if she were part of them: 'It was so intoxicating and I felt so alive' (Lawson 1998, p.2).

Donna Williams describes how she could 'feel' colours:

> These streetlights were yellow with a hint of pink but in a buzz state they were an intoxicating iridescent-like pink-yellow. My mind dived deeper and deeper into the colour, trying to feel its nature and become it as I progressively lost sense of self in its overwhelming presence. Each of the colours resonated different feelings within me and it was like they played me as a chord, where other colours played one note at a time.
>
> It had been the same as long as I had known...some things hadn't changed...since I was an infant swept up in the perception of swirling air particles, a child lost in the repetition of a pattern of sound, or a teenager staring for hours at coloured billiard balls, trying to grasp the experience of the particular colour I was climbing into. (Williams 1999, p.19)

Willey (1999) loved the sensation that came from floating with water: she felt as if she was liquid, tranquil, smooth.

In the state of 'resonance' one can sense the surface, texture and density of material without looking at it with physical eyes or touching it with physical hands or tasting it with a physical tongue or tapping it to hear how it sounds, i.e. sensing it with non-physical senses (the so-called 'shadow senses') (Williams 1999). Those who experience this condition can be 'in resonance' with colours, sounds, objects, places, plants, animals, people. For example:

> I could resonate with the cat and spent hours lying in front of it, making no physical contact with it. I could resonate with the tree in the park and feel myself merge with its size, its stability, its calm and its flow. (Williams 1998, p.44)

'In resonance' with people they can sense ('see', 'hear' etc.) thoughts, emotions, pain, etc. of other people, for example:

> It is rare that I know what anyone is actually thinking, but concurrent emotions are very common. (McKean 1994)

> When I was younger I heard a lot of noises in my head, spoken things and unspoken things. Tell me you can hear people think. I wish I didn't. If there is a medication that will kill people's thoughts I like (sic) to try it. (Walker and Cantello 1994)

> I physically felt the pain when someone banged themselves. Around someone with a broken leg, I felt their pain in my leg. (Williams 1998, p.59)

> I...remember responding to people's call by coming into the room, sometimes answering their request by going and getting what they'd wanted. People had seemed surprised at these behaviours because they hadn't been verbally called or asked or that I was busy with things of my own at the time. (Williams 1998, p.27)

A woman with Asperger syndrome describes how she 'feels' people: 'I know when people do not like me, or find me strange and scary, no matter how polite and friendly they try to look. I just *physically* feel their attitude to me.' Similar experiences have been reported by few other autistic individuals. Probably, some people are reluctant to share these experiences because there is always a fear to be considered 'psychic'.

Interestingly, cats and dogs seem to possess the similar sort of 'telepathic' ability. Sheldrake (1999) suggests it could be caused by some force field ('morphic field') that is not yet fully understood. Donna Williams (1998) offers her explanation of the phenomenon: the body is more than a physical form. It is also an energy form. Some people's energy boundaries are more 'open' than for most people. These are the people most prone to a wider range of 'psychic' experiences and 'déjà vu'. This state is involuntary, beyond their control. They can either give in to it or try to fight it.

What to look for:

These experiences are very difficult for 'outsiders' to identify. There are several reasons:

- Even high-functional verbal autistic children often see no need to describe these experiences as they assume that others experience the same.

- Autistic adults are often very unwilling to talk about these in order not to sound crazy or psychic.

However, many parents do feel that their children are able to 'read their minds' (not to be confused with the 'Theory of Mind'), but they are afraid to articulate their suspicions. Indeed, I have met two mothers who confided in me about their feelings. Other indicators can be:

1. Seems to be absorbed with lights, colours, sounds, smells, etc.

2. Seems to feel pain of others

3. Seems to be absorbed with body movements

4. Appears to be in constant motion

Daydreaming

It is not uncommon among autistic people to experience so-called 'day-dreams'. Whether this phenomenon is the sixth sense, clairvoyance, precognition or another form of extra-sensory perception and whether we can explain it or not, it does exist. Personal accounts of autistic individuals contain quite a number of these experiences, for example:

> At school strange things were happening. I would have daydreams in which I was watching children I knew. I would see them doing the trivialest of things: peeling potatoes over the sink, getting themselves a peanut butter sandwich before going to bed. Such daydreams were like films in which I'd see a sequence of everyday events, which really didn't relate in any way to myself. I began to test the truth of these daydreams; approaching the friends I'd seen in them and asking them to give me a step-by-step detailed picture of what they were doing at the time I had the daydream. Amazingly, to the finest detail, I had been right. This was nothing I had controlled, it simply came into my head, but it frightened me. (Williams 1992, p.63)

> There were odd occasions at school when I seemed to know things about people before they did. One day when two children were skipping rope and the game was getting intense, I knew that one child would fall down – I had hardly seen the thought when it happened. I know this could easily be coincidence, but it happened many times. Sometimes I would dream of a place, in great detail, and then experience that very same place at some future time. (Lawson 1998, p.30)

Donna Williams emphasizes that these are not fantasies, these are real experiences, which she calls 'unintentional out-of-body experiences':

> In my teens I lived in quite a dangerous and lonely state a lot of the time and this caused me to 'visit' non-physically people and places where I felt safe. I didn't fantasize what I'd like to say or do. I simply found myself feeling physically in these places or with these people... Yet I did feel myself moving up the stairs to my friend's flat, through the front door and into the kitchen. I could sense the smell of the room and the noises in the room. I could 'hear' and 'see' as my friends moved about and went on with things. (Williams 1998, p.34)

What to look for:

There are no general indications to this phenomenon. However, bearing in mind that it is possible, one might find that some behaviours or attempts to explain something 'just fit'.

> *As the expressive language of the children is limited, it is difficult to say whether they experience this. Though, sometimes, Vicky's mother 'feels' that her daughter 'reads' her emotions, no matter how hard she tries to hide them.*

Chapter 5

Cognitive Styles

> I struggled to use 'the world' language to describe a way of thinking
> and being and experiencing for which this world gives you no words
> or concepts... (Williams 1994, p.84)

As the way a person perceives the world affects the way he stores and
utilizes information, we will discuss information processing problems and
differences in autism considering different cognitive styles; analysing
discrete functions specific to autism, such as attention, memory, concept
formation, categorizing/generalizing, types of thinking, imagination.

Subconscious, unconscious and preconscious cognitive processes

- Conscious mind implies the mental faculties are awake and
  active.

- Subconscious mind can be defined as part of the mental field
  outside the range of attention, and therefore outside
  consciousness.

- Unconscious mind comprises those mental processes whose
  existence is inferred from their effects.

- Preconscious mind contains ideas or memories that can be
  readily be made conscious.

The conscious mind is not the only way of receiving information about the
world. Even without conscious awareness we still continue to experience
things and accumulate information. Thus, even unconscious people (for

example, patients under anaesthesia) can hear conversations around them, remember them and even repeat them later on (Ratey 2001). Research on blindsight has established that unconscious processing can occur in the absence of conscious realization of visual images (Cowey and Stoerig 1991; Weiskrantz 1986).

We are limited in our ability to process information consciously. However, subconsciously and/or preconsciously it is possible to take an infinite amount of information as we do not have to filter and interpret it. Donna Williams (1994; 1998) describes the process of receiving knowledge from subconscious to preconscious to conscious, where the subconscious mind is a storeroom containing uninterpreted information that is still accumulated within preconsciousness where it can be processed later removed from its context, and becomes triggered voluntarily or involuntarily and is perceived consciously after it has been expressed – 'sort of listening in on oneself' (Williams 1998).

Preconscious (indirect) style versus conscious (direct) style

There seem to be two distinct styles of accumulating information, which differ in ways of perceiving, storing and retrieving information. The first one is a preconscious style ('a waking subconscious mind' – Williams 1998) receiving an infinite amount of unprocessed information which is literal and objective, indirectly, without conscious interpretation. The storing capacity is also unlimited. However, the access and retrieval of this information is difficult: it can be triggered but not accessed voluntarily (Williams 1998). Research (Farah and Feinberg 1997; Gazzaniga 1988) has shown that different neural mechanisms appear to be involved in conscious and unconscious processing.

Some autistic people use the preconscious system to take in information. They use their senses peripherally. It allows them to take in a great amount of information though they themselves are 'absent' from the process. That is, they do not know what information they have accumulated, though it may be triggered from the outside and they surprise us (and often themselves) with their knowledge we have never thought they have. It is sort of 'unknown knowing' (Williams 1996). They might accumulate as much as 95 per cent of information preconsciously, without learning (Williams 1994).

Dr Robyn Young, a psychologist at Finders University in Adelaide, conducted very interesting experiments. Using a technique called transcranial magnetic stimulation to switch off the frontal temporal lobe (the thinking part of the brain), the researcher tested the savant skills in volunteers. Five out of seventeen volunteers showed improvements in memory, calendar calculating and drawing abilities. Young hypothesizes that we all have the potential to develop skills that we did not know we had. By shutting off the conscious part of the brain we can enter the unconscious domain. However, there were serious side-effects. It appears that those who undergo such a brain bombardment lose many abilities as well as gaining some, for example, one person got lost on his way to work the day after the experiment.

Nadia could draw as a professional artist at the age of three. But she was autistic and could not communicate. The more she learned how to communicate and the more 'normal' her functioning became, the more 'ordinary' became her drawing. She developed language but lost her 'gift'. However, some autistic individuals do not 'lose' their gift with their social development (for instance, Stephen Wiltshire) but use it as a 'key' to open the door to the social world around it.

Some autistic people take in information consciously and directly but at the cost of its coherence, because they have to narrow their attention and shut down any background information in order to cope with conscious processing of whatever is in the focus of their attention. Some autistic people seem to fluctuate between these two styles.

By distinguishing between preconscious and conscious perceptual processing, we can distinguish between different types of intelligence – conscious and preconscious, the latter with little conscious awareness ('unknown knowing').

Attention in autism

Sensory issues and attentional issues are most likely both real and both primary; in some cases one may help cause the other, but I suspect that they are usually related only through similar neurobiodevelopmental causes. Both attentional and sensory problems may have developmental consequences that help to create the full autistic syndrome. (Blackburn 1999, p.7)

The ability to attend selectively to meaningful stimuli while ignoring irrelevant ones is essential to cognitive functioning (Lane and Pearson 1982). As we have discussed earlier, filtering of an infinite amount of information is necessary to make processing of information effective and conscious. Consciously we can process only a limited amount of stimuli, and the decision on which stimuli are to be processed in each situation is of paramount importance. Impaired selective attention results in increased distraction and diminished cognitive functioning, because responses to irrelevant stimuli interfere with the processing of targeted information (Douglas and Peters 1979; Lane and Pearson 1982).

Some researchers define selective attention as a component of directed attention (Davies 1983; Posner 1975). According to their model, directed attention includes:

- a selective process for distinguishing the relevant from the irrelevant

- an intensive process for the distribution of different amounts of attention across a set of stimuli, depending on their value

- an alerting and sustaining process that involves vigilance, i.e. the energy to sustain attention.

Ornitz (1989) adds a motor component to these perceptual processes, enabling and modulating perceptual activity (for example, visual scanning). Impairments or distortions of any of these components may result in neglect. Ornitz hypothesizes that autistic behaviour can be better understood as a disorder of directed attention involving neurophysiological mechanisms primarily, though not necessarily exclusively, in the right hemisphere.

It is widely reported that autistic children appear to ignore relevant stimuli in favour of apparently meaningless stimuli in their environment. But we should remember that the decision which stimuli are relevant and which are meaningless depends on the common stock of experiences and knowledge. Autistic people might attend to what *they* think important, but usually it turns out to be different from what non-autistic people think is important (Rand), and described as 'idiosyncratic focus of attention'.

Uta Frith (1989) applies the theory of weak central coherence in autism to account for this idiosyncratic attentional focus. A good decision about what to attend to would be based on large amounts of pooled information, and if coherence at this central decision-making point is weak, the direction of attention would be quite haphazard.

Blamires (1999) offers an alternative explanation to 'central coherence'. He suggests that people with autism attribute different meaning to stimuli or ignore them as meaningless because they possess a different stock of knowledge about the world from non-autistic people. It is the stock of knowledge that dictates what aspects of the environment are important. This view coincides with relevance theory introduced by Sperber and Wilson (1986): our attention automatically turns to what seems relevant in the environment.

Brad Rand, an autistic person, confirms this view, as he picks what he thinks important, but usually it turns out to be different from what non-autistic people focus on in the situation. As he has tunnel vision, everything that is not at focus of his attention at the moment fades out. It would be helpful for a person with this attention pattern to be told explicitly what to look at or what to listen to, to create a shared attentional focus.

Patterns of attention in autism

In order to avoid sensory information overload, autistic people acquire voluntary and involuntary strategies and compensations, such as mono-processing, when they focus their attention to one single channel, or so-called 'tunnel perception', when they concentrate on a detail instead of a whole. They have very narrowly focused attention. Autistic individuals often compare this attentional pattern with having 'a mind like a flashlight', 'a laser pointer' or 'a laser beam' that highlights only a single dot (an area of high focus) that they see very clearly while everything around it is grey and fuzzy (Blackburn 1999; O'Neill 1999; Rand undated). Murray (1992) refers to this phenomenon in monotropism as 'attention tunnelling'.

Rimland (1978) believes that the various forms of autism represent severe disorders of the attentional mechanism. The author assumes that autistic savants' attentional mechanisms are pathologically locked at the indistractable, superintense end of the concentration scale. In Rimland's view an autistic savant is endowed with the capacity to deal with minute details at the cost of being unaware of the background or context of the detail: he is able to *apprehend* visual or auditory stimuli but not to *comprehend* them.

We may try to imagine the problems a narrow attention focus might create in autism by conducting a simple experiment. Cover a picture (of a portrait/an object/a scene, etc.) with a sheet of paper with a small hole in the centre. Ask somebody to recognize what is on the picture by moving the sheet with a hole in any direction. The difficulty of recognition with a narrow focus is obvious.

Another problem autistic children experience is difficulty in switching attention. For many of them shifting attention from one stimulus to the other is a relatively slow process that results in a sort of pause or delay of reaction. This 'too slow attention switching' process may be caused by delayed processing of each stimulus. Recent research (Courchesne *et al.* 1994) has provided some evidence that a simple delay in attention-switching might account for many behaviours associated with autism.

In contrast to Attention Deficit Hyperactivity Disorder (ADHD), which is characterized by short attention span, autism exhibits other deviant attentional patterns such as problems in selectivity, too narrow focus and slow shifting speed. One of the consequences of this is that autistic people often see things in fragments, disconnected. However, autism and ADHD can often overlap: people with autism may be very hyper and have a short attention span, while individuals with ADHD can exhibit autistic traits (Blakemore-Brown 2001).

There is some evidence that lack of Theory of Mind in many autistic people is probably the result of their problems with attention-shifting, their inability to attend to multiple cues.

The most common attentional problem in autism is the failure of autistic people to establish and maintain joint attention, i.e. the ability to attend to the same stimuli as the other person. That leads to the failure to share experiences. As a joint attention task involves a divided attention task when a person should attend to both the object of the joint attention and the person with whom the experience should be shared, an autistic person often fails to monitor both of these (if he works in 'mono' or has 'tunnel vision') and either fails to attend to the object of joint attention or to the other person's shifts of attention. This results in the failure to comprehend the meaning of the interaction and hinders social and cultural development.

For learning language, joint attention is essential. A child connects a new word with the object of joint attention. A deficit in joint attention affects the way autistic children learn new concepts. They may hear the word and remember it in connection with either a part of the object they are attending to at the moment, or the whole object (different from the object of joint attention but at their 'flashlight'), or even the whole scene (gestalt perception), or sensation they are experiencing at the moment. Kanner (1946) describes the case of a child who always associated the phrase 'Peter eater' with saucepans. The explanation lies in the way the boy 'learned' the phrase: his mother was saying this nursery rhyme in the kitchen when she accidentally dropped a saucepan. The boy connected the phrase with a saucepan and 'learned' it.

The main thing is not to assume that autistic children will always pick the same thing as we might do. For example, a teacher shows a picture of a car: 'This is a car', but a child might focus on the reflection of light on the teacher's earring and 'learns' the word with his private meaning; another child might feel itchy and refer the teacher's comment 'this is a car' to the sensation he is feeling at the moment. In this case, all instructions should be explicit ('Look at what I am looking/what I am holding', etc.); the child should be given enough time to switch attention from what he was doing to you, and then to the object you are talking about. If he looks in the same direction as you do, do not assume he sees the same thing. Always try to 'see' from the child's perspective (his perceptual and cognitive patterns).

Autistic people are reported often not to notice other people because for them, people seem no more important (or even less) than objects. If they have perceptual problems, people 'look like shapes, like furniture and trees are shapes' and are not different 'from any other sight or sound' (Rand, undated, p.9). Autistic children appear to ignore people or use them as 'tools' to get what they want. The explanation for this can be that because of attentional and perceptual problems autistic children are unable to divide their attention between the object they want and the person 'on their way' and process separate 'pieces of information' (the person and the object, or even parts of them) simultaneously. In this case they do not 'perceive' the person as a person or notice the presence of the person at all.

It is a typical description of autistic children that they are asking for something (the phrases they have been taught to use) in an empty room, i.e. addressing nobody. The child might concentrate all his attention and energy on the learned phrase and performing it, and he cannot simultaneously appreciate that there should be someone to whom he is supposed to address the request.

Memory in autism

The main characteristics of 'autistic memory' are gestalt and literalness. Oliver Sacks notes that in such a memory there tends to be an immovable connection of scene and time, of content and context (a so-called concrete situational or episodic memory) that results in the astounding powers of literal recall so common in autistic savants, along with difficulty extracting the salient features from these particular memories, in order to build a general sense and memory. The author describes this type of memory as quasi-mechanical – 'like a vast store, or library, or archive – not even indexed or categorized, or held together by association, yet where anything might be accessed in an instant, as in the random-access memory of a computer' (Sacks 1995, p.208).

Many people with autism do not remember verbally but while remembering they actually see, hear, feel, smell or taste the items (in their mind). The thought about something produces real experiences they had when encountering this thing or event for the first time. They store their visual, auditory, olfactory, gustatory and tactile memories, which are very real. For instance, the thought of textures they hate might cause goose bumps and chills and a general sense of unease would follow (Willey 1999).

Most commonly reported are the feats of visual and auditory memory. Well-known pictures by Stephen Wiltshire, an autistic savant, of architectural buildings, contain the smallest details such as style and size of windows, and this is despite the fact that he saw the original buildings only once for a few minutes and did not begin his drawings immediately. It is so-called eidetic or photographic memory, which allows these people to create visualizations that are as intense as those brought about by the original stimuli (Carter 1998).

Some researchers (Rose 1993) suggest that up to 50 per cent of five-year-olds have the ability to 'see' an imagined image as though it was really there. Some adults are reported to retain this ability (see, for example, Schatzman 1980). Clara Park (1967) says that her autistic daughter's eye is like a camera: she draws pictures of houses very accurately, with finest detail. Temple Grandin (1996a) writes about Barbara, a woman with autism, whose ability to recognize pattern has made her one of the best technicians in the laboratory identifying cancer cells. Her visual abilities enable her to spot abnormal cells instantly, because they 'just jump out at her'.

Some autistic individuals are reported to be able to spell excellently thanks to their visual/photographic memory: as they read they quickly memorize the spellings of words; when they misspell a word they can refer to their mental catalogue of data to recall which spelling looks more accurate (O'Neill 1999). Temple Grandin (1996a, p.24) compares her process of remembering things with a computer: 'I store information in my head as if it were on a CD-ROM disc. When I recall something I have learned, I replay the video in my imagination.' Her memory patterns are similar to those described by A. R. Luria (1987) who studied a man with amazing feats of memory: when the man heard or read a word, it was at once converted into a visual image corresponding with the object the word signified for him.

Some autistic people, while having excellent memory, have problems with recognition memory; for example, Jared Blackburn has trouble recognizing faces, letters and objects without actively visualizing them (Blackburn 1999).

Some have a very good auditory memory ('sound memory', 'audiographic memory' – Williams 1996), that enables them to repeat ('replay') long strings of things they have heard. Some can record musical pieces in their minds, then hum or play them flawlessly on an instrument later on (O'Neill 1999). Some can 'hear' conversations in their memory (Willey 1999) or even whole 'sound situations'. 'It is like replaying a tape recording of conversations, songs heard and so on' (Williams 1998). They seem to have 'audio tapes' in their memory with detailed 'sound pictures' of objects, people, events.

Some autistic people store 'smell images' in their memory.

Despite their excellent rote memory many autistic people are very forgetful. This is another paradox out of many in autism: on the one hand, they have an inability to forget (Luria 1987), on the other hand they may be very forgetful. For instance, they may forget what they need to buy at the shop, but they are unable to forget the clothes someone was wearing or the arrangement of the furniture in the house they moved from many years ago.

Jordan and Powell (1995) consider the main memory difficulty in autism as the failure to develop a personal memory for episodes, i.e. the failure to experience self as a part of events that leads to a difficulty in developing personal memories. They can remember things but they may fail to remember these things happening to them. In order to recall they need to be prompted with specific cues.

Ways to access memory (types of memory retrievals)

Many autistic people are unable to recall memories unless they are triggered. They often cannot voluntarily 'get access' to their stored information. However, if cued or prompted with particular words, intonation, gestures, or surroundings they may astonish their parents (and even themselves) with the knowledge they have accumulated. They seem to have no conscious control on their 'database' and are dependent on the 'right triggers'.

Snyder and Mitchell (1999) hypothesize that in contrast to low-functioning autistic people, autistic savants may have 'privileged access' to their memory which allows them to produce outstanding results in art, music, calculation. They are able to create their works by directly accessing 'primary memory areas' at lower levels of information.

Associative memory

Autistic memory is often described as associative memory (or 'serial memory' – Williams 1996). It differs from 'ordinary' (verbal memory) in the way it unfolds: verbal memory is linear, associative memory is non-linear (Grandin 1996a), multi-dimensional, sort of 'spatial', and can be triggered by sensory stimuli, such as smells, certain colours or patterns, touch, physical movement, combination of sounds or words. For example, the word 'under' triggered Temple Grandin to picture herself getting under the cafeteria tables at school during an air-raid drill. Then she continued to 'play video' of the teacher scolding her after she hit Alfred for putting dirt on her shoe, and then 'saw' submarines under the Antarctic and the Beatles song 'Yellow Submarine'. If she let her mind pause on the picture of the yellow submarine, she then heard the song; then she would start humming the song. When she got to the part about people coming on board, her association would switch to the gangway of a ship she had seen in Australia, etc. (Grandin 1996a). Seeing the black and white stripes on a toy plane can trigger the memory of eating humbugs in a classroom many years before and might run into who was in the class on that day and what was being taught and the noise that the book made when snapped closed and the exact path the teacher travelled across the room at a particular point, etc. (Williams 1996). Touching the doorway to a room may trigger the serial memory of touching the same door of the same room another time and the events that happened after this (Williams 1996). Temple Grandin (2000) compares this type of memory with a Web browser: a Web browser finds specific words; by analogy, autistic people look for memories (pictural, auditory, etc.) that are associated with the words they hear or say.

Many autistic children use this serial/associative memory as a compensation for their inability to process information quickly (delayed processing): they do not process information at the time it happens, they respond to the situation 'from memory' when something remembered in a serial way is triggered. They often cannot keep track of conversation as in the short break between two halves of a sentence, there may have been triggered a huge number of tracks, leading to tracks, leading to tracks (Williams 1996). They just cannot stop endless associations (Grandin

1996a) and often use songs, commercials, etc. to respond, or use idiosyncratic routinized responses.

> *'Alex, do you want broccoli?' (The boy hates it.)*
> *'Yes, please.'*
> *Mother puts the plate with broccoli on the table in front of him.*
> *Alex screams and with a very loud 'No!' rushes out of the kitchen.*

Concept formation. Categorization. Generalization

Before language, the symbol (concept) formation process operates in sensory modalities. The aspects of perceived experience are stored in long-term memory and form sort of 'perceptual symbols' files, to be used later for reference. From vision, visual images are acquired. From hearing, auditory perceptual symbols are stored. From olfaction, 'smell pictures' are received. From gustation, a file of 'tastes' is filled in. From touch perceptual symbols for textures, pressure and temperatures are formed. And from proprioception, perceptual symbols for limb movements and body positions are mapped. The neuroscience research indicates that each type of perceptual symbol is accomplished and stored in its respective brain areas. If some areas are damaged, conceptualization of this particular modality becomes disrupted (Damasio and Damasio 1994; Gainotti *et al.* 1995). By the pre-verbal stage of concept formation, autistic children exhibit differences. As sensory dysfunction is present (whatever form it may take), perceptual symbols in autism will differ from non-autistic ones. The symbol formation process in autism often depends on the channel(s) the person uses, or which particular channel is 'on-line' at the moment. As a result of differences in perception (such as described in Chapters 3 and 4) the information about objects, people and events is not organized into a coherent picture. That is why perceptual images (of any modality) are not established into categories and remain as separate entities. Thus, different perceptual systems develop different conceptual systems and result in different intelligence systems.

With the appearance of language, the concept formation system changes. Any word generalizes. 'Labels' enable us to categorize and generalize. We may 'file' our mind with representations of the outside world, and easily operate with them creating new ideas. The content of a linguistic symbol (a word) does not resemble its referent. In contrast perceptual 'words' refer clearly to specific objects, states, events. Because autistic 'words' contain different perceptual content, they are not functionally equivalent to non-autistic concepts. Autistic 'words' are very concrete and specific. Instead of storing general meanings of things and events (which is a prerogative of a verbal language) they construct sensory perceptual mental images. They store the *experiences* (sensory impressions/templates). Once a perceptual image is stored in long-term memory, it becomes a representation of physical input. It becomes a symbol for a certain referent and can represent the object in its absence. It means that if a person has stored 'a ball' by smell, then if it does not have the same smell as the one he stored for the first time, it cannot be identified as 'a ball', even if it looks like a ball, sounds like a ball, etc. To be identified, the thing should 'feel right', i.e. be exactly the same as in the first experience. Thus, autistic people store sensory impressions (taste, smell, colour, shape, feel, etc.) which they use later for reference and 'identification'.

Tito, an autistic boy, could not find any association between things that change places. He could identify a picture of a dog on the book as a dog, but a dog in the park could not be identified. It took years, and a lot of practice by him and the patience of his mother who kept asking him questions, comparing pictures of a dog and a cow with the living animals on the road (Mukhopadhyay 1999).

This phenomenon is brilliantly described by Donna Williams:

> I would learn how to tackle a given situation in one context but be lost when confronted by the same situation in another context. Things just didn't translate. If I learned something while I was standing with a woman in a kitchen and it was summer and it was daytime, the lesson wouldn't be triggered in a similar situation if I was standing with a man in another room and it was winter and it was nighttime. Things were stored but the compulsive overcategorization of them was so refined that events had to be closed to identical to be considered comparable. (Williams 1994, p.62)

Paradoxically, sometimes different stimuli may 'feel' the same and become 'unconventional personal synonyms'. For example, to Donna Williams some words have a similar shape, pattern or rhythms without being similar in meaning, e.g. 'Margaret' and 'Elizabeth' have the same feel and seem similar to her (Williams 1996). To Alex, an autistic boy, the words 'Oliver' and 'cinema' are the same.

What to look for:

1. Displays a good visual/auditory/gustatory/olfactory/tactile/kinaesthetic memory

2. Reactions are triggered by some stimuli (lights, colours, sounds, words, textures, smells, movements, etc.)

3. Uses songs, commercials, etc. to respond

4. Uses idiosyncratic routinized responses

5. Cannot keep track of conversation

Alex displays a very good visual and auditory memory. John is good at recognizing 'smell messages'. Vicky can distinguish the slightest difference between very similar textures.

Helen can start reciting poems, triggered by one word, then 'jumps' to the recollection of her visit to her grandma, triggered by the word in the poem, etc. It is very difficult to keep her 'on track'.

Perceptual thinking

There appear to be two basic types of thinking in autistic people: totally perceptual (usually visual) thinkers and the music, math and memory thinkers (Grandin 1999). Research findings (Farah 1989; Zeki 1992) show that verbal and visual thinking work via different brain systems. These studies reveal that in brain-damaged patients one system can be damaged, while another system may be normal. In autism, the systems that process visual-spatial information are intact (Grandin 1996b). The research on frontal temporal lobe dementia has provided scientific evidence for the idea of hidden visual thinking under a layer of verbal thinking (Grandin 2000).

One of the characteristics of autism is the remarkable ability of most autistic people to excel at visual-spatial skills while performing very poorly at verbal skills. For those who have visual thinking ('thinking in pictures' – Grandin 1996a), words are like a second language; their thought processes are different from language-based thinkers. Temple Grandin, for example, translates both spoken and written words into full-colour movies, complete with sound, which run 'like a VCR tape' in her head (Grandin 1996a). When she lectures, the language is 'downloaded' out of memory from files that are like tape recordings. To describe the process Temple Grandin uses the computer analogy:

> I use slides or notes to trigger opening the different files. When I am talking about something for the first time, I look at the visual images on the 'computer monitor' in my imagination, then the language part of me describes those images. After I have given the lecture several times, the new material in language is switched over into 'audio tape-recording files'. (Grandin 2000)

The ideas are expressed as images for visual thinkers. They can take things apart and put them together in different designs completely in their imagination. They can manipulate images to solve most problems. Jared Blackburn, for instance, can often measure objects by visualizing a ruler moving along the object (Blackburn 1999). 'Visual thinkers' actually *see* their thoughts. Things happen like a movie in their minds, to provide a concrete basis for understanding what is going on around them (O'Neill 1999). Jasmine O'Neill, a non-verbal woman with autism who has established herself as a talented writer, musician and illustrator, can see the colour and feel the texture of her emotions against her 'mind's eye like a projector' (O'Neill 2000).

'Visual thinkers' often have difficulty with long verbal information, and prefer written texts:

> When I read, I translate written words into color movies or simply store a photo of the written page to be read later. When I retrieve the material I see a photocopy of the page in my imagination. (Grandin 1996a, p.31)

Visual thinking is very fast, and not sequential. Very often autistic people have poor auditory short-term memory. They have difficulty in remembering auditory instructions consisting of three or more steps. However, when these instructions are presented in 'visual steps' – pictures, photographs, etc. it is much easier for them, as it helps them to 'translate' from 'auditory' into their internal visual mode.

Autistic children usually learn nouns first, as nouns are easily associated with pictures in their minds. Words that have no concrete visual meaning, such as 'put', or 'on', or 'over', have no meaning for them until they have a visual image to fix them in the memory (Grandin 1996a, b; Park 1967). For example, Donna Williams became frustrated when she could not find an 'of' button on her calculator to calculate percentages. To understand verbs and adverbs Temple Grandin has learned to visualize them:

> The word 'jumping' triggered a memory of jumping hurdles at the mock Olympics held at my elementary school. Adverbs often trigger inappropriate images – 'quickly' reminds me of Nestle's Quik – unless they are paired with a verb, which modifies my visual image… As a child, I left out words such as 'is', 'the', and 'it', because they had no meaning by themselves. Similarly, words like 'of' and 'an' made no sense… To this day certain verb conjugations, such as 'to be', are absolutely meaningless to me. (Grandin 1996a, pp.30, 31)

Autistic people have trouble with words that cannot be constructed into a mental picture. Ron Davis has identified 'trigger words' which cannot be mentally 'seen', such as 'the', 'of', 'for' (Davis 1997).

To get the idea of how they might hear (create mental understanding through producing mental images), read the passage below in which all unimaginable (i.e. incomprehensible for them) words are omitted, and try to imagine how confusing it might be for an autistic child:

> *Alex…tidy…room Look…sister's room…see…nice girl…people say…want…say…lazy boy…go…room…help…tidy…*
>
> *[Alex, why don't you tidy up your room? Look at your sister's room. Everything is in order. Everybody can see what a nice girl she is. And*

what would people say about you? You don't want them to say that you are a lazy boy, do you? Let's go to your room and I will help you to tidy it up.]

However, visualization thinking patterns are different from one person to the other. Some 'visualizers' can search the memory pictures like searching slides and can stop on any picture to study. They are able to control the rate at which pictures 'flash' through their imagination. Some people are unable to control the rate and end up with overloaded images coming all at once. Still others are slow to interpret the information. Thus, for a 'visual thinker', not being able to visualize quickly what is said, or mentally hold visual images together, means that verbal messages are not translated and remained meaningless. That is why autistic people often have problems learning abstract things that cannot be thought about in pictures. To understand abstract concepts they use visual images. For example, to understand personal relationships some autistic individuals used the image of sliding doors (Grandin 1996a, b; Park and Youderian 1974).

Besides, the 'quality' of visual thinking may depend on the state the person is in, and even the time of the day. For instance, for Temple Grandin (2000) pictures are clearer and with the most detailed images when she is drifting off to sleep; her language part of the brain is completely shut off at night.

Visual thinkers, as a rule, can pass simple 'Theory of Mind' (understanding other people's thoughts and intentions) tests as they can visualize what the other person would see. As for more complex 'Theory of Mind' tasks, the problem is often with the short-term working memory and not with their lack of 'Theory of Mind'. For example, Temple Grandin can solve these tests if she is allowed to write down the sequence of events (Grandin 1999).

Not all people with autism are highly visual thinkers. They appear to be on a continuum of visualization skills ranging from next to none, to seeing vague generalized pictures, to seeing semi-specific pictures, to seeing, as in the case of Temple Grandin, in very specific pictures (Grandin 1996a). Unlike most people who think from general to specific, 'visual thinkers' move from video-like, specific images to generalization and concepts, for example:

...my concept of dogs is inextricably linked to every dog I've ever known. It's as if I have a card catalogue of dogs I have seen, complete with pictures which continually grows as I add more examples to my video library. (Grandin 1996a, p.28)

'Perceptual thinkers' can experience thought as reality. It means that when they think about something, they relive it visually, auditorily, etc. and emotionally. O'Neill (1999) compares it with 'watching a movie: a mind-movie' – the pictures of thoughts in this movie 'transport you and create emotions as you view scenes'. It is not uncommon to see an autistic child giggling to himself. One of the reasons might be that the child relives some funny moment, using recorded, stored sensory images. What is very difficult for the parents to comprehend (and accept) is that a child might laugh or giggle non-stop when someone is crying. It might be one of the defensive strategies used by the child – when he is sad he tries to lessen it by 'feeling the cheerful emotions of a happy mind-movie' (O'Neill 1999).

Perceptual thinking can account for some language idiosyncrasies, observed by Frith (1989), such as that an autistic child may say 'French toast' when he is happy, etc.

Some autistic people who are not visual thinkers may think in 'audio tape clips': instead of using visual images, they operate with specific audio clips (Grandin 2000). They 'see' better with their ears as they store 'audio pictures' with detailed sound information, and 'read' these audio texts. For 'auditory thinkers' sound signals are much easier to understand than any visual ones, such as body postures, facial expressions and gestures.

The examples of gustatory and olfactory images can be 'gustatory/olfactory hallucinations', reported by some autistic people.

In all the cases, a whole or gestalt is visualized/heard, etc. and the details are added in a non-sequential manner. For example, when Temple Grandin designs equipment, she often has a general outline of the system, and then each section of it becomes clear as she adds details (Grandin, 2000).

Perceptual thinking may be a slow method of thinking as it takes time to 'play the video/listen to the tape', etc.

What to look for:

1. Easily solves jigsaw puzzles

2. Remembers routes and places

3. Memorizes enormous amounts of information at a glance

4. Poor at mathematics

5. Learns nouns first

6. Has difficulties with adverbs and prepositions

7. Idiosyncratic patterns in language development, e.g. names one thing to denote the other, etc.

8. Composes musical pieces, songs, 'sound pictures'

9. Complains about being touched/wearing certain clothes/heat/cold when the stimuli are not present

10. Complains about smells/tastes in the absence of the stimuli

11. Mimics actions when instructions are being given

12. Experiences movement while being still (e.g. 'I am flying' while being in bed)

> *John and Helen are very good at jigsaw puzzles. Helen can easily solve a jigsaw puzzle of 120 pieces even if the picture is upside-down. Alex, Helen and Vicky easily memorize enormous amounts of information at a glance (though its reproduction should be properly triggered, e.g. instructions given by the same person with the same intonation, etc.).*

'Inertia' (executive function deficit)

Another problem autistic people are reported to experience is 'inertia' (Dekker 1999) – difficulty in starting and planning the task. But once they start, they find it hard to stop until they finish.

Autistic people tend to be rigid and inflexible, perserverative, narrowly focused on details and deficient in the ability to inhibit familiar or overlearned responses (Ozonoff *et al.* 1994). For example, Alex cannot stop doing something until he has finished the task, no matter how tired he is. He will cry and exhibit some destructive behaviours (kicking the chair, throwing things from the table) but continue with the task until he completes it.

Alternatively, some autistic children may have difficulty persisting at the task and move quickly to something else and something else and something else. Deficits in planning, inhibition of prepotent responses, flexibility, and working memory are known as deficits in executive functioning. Executive functioning impairment has been proposed as a potential underlying deficit of autism because the symptoms demonstrated by patients with prefrontal cortical dysfunction are similar to autistic behaviours (Ozonoff, Roger and Pennington 1991). One difficulty with this hypothesis is that autism is not the only disorder with potential executive function impairment and further research is needed to find out how executive function deficits in autism differ from those of other disorders.

Deficits in executive function are reflected in speech and language impairments. For non-autistic people this process seems to be almost automatic. However, for a person with executive function deficit it is a difficult process including many stages to come through. Thus a thought has to be held in working memory while the response is being organized and produced. Autistic children may have something to say, but they have difficulty in finding the words they want, getting them formed and produced. Generally they have less difficulty in familiar environments, with familiar persons, in familiar situations, but they may not be able to do it in other environments, with unfamiliar people or situations, though they know how to do it.

Imagination

One of the diagnostic characteristics of autism is a lack or impairment of imagination. Yet autistic individuals do not agree with this description. There are many examples of 'unimpaired imagination' to be found in beautifully written prose or poetry full of poetic images, drawings, painings, equipment created by people who are supposed to lack imagination.

Imagination is defined as a mental faculty forming images of external objects not present to the senses; creative faculty of the mind. The differences in perception and memorizing information inevitably bring differences in imagination.

The quality of memory influences our ability to imagine. We do not remember things in detail; we fill in the blanks by imagining the details. The better the memory, the poorer the imagination. This paradox has attracted attention of many researchers. Langdon Down (1887) noted that extraordinary memory is often combined with great impairments in reasoning power. Sir Francis Galton, one of the founders of the field psychology stated that scientists in general have poor imagery. He specifically highlighted the antagonism between sharp mental imagery and abstract thought. The memory of autistic people is too good. However, they do possess imaginative abilities. Oliver Sacks (1995) noticed that Stephen Wiltshire's drawings, though accurate in some ways, contained additions, subtractions, revisions, etc. They by no means resembled copies or photographs, and always showed Stephen's peculiar style. A more precise definition of impairments in imagination, therefore, would be that imagination in autism is qualitatively different from non-autistic imagination. Autistic people find it difficult to invent stories or conversations (non-autistic characteristic of creativity) but they may be very creative in 'solving better defined problems' (Blackburn 1999). They can write poetry and prose filled with graphic images 'inside' their head and then type, speak, sing or play it (Kochmeister 1995).

We cannot deny the imaginative powers and creativity that enables them to write poetry and prose, to invent equipment, compose music, etc. And another proof of imagination in autism is that many autistic individuals try really hard to imagine how non-autistic people experience the world, think and feel. (Why don't we use our imagination in order to understand these people?)

Chapter 6

Other Sensory Conditions

There are other sensory related conditions which appear to be quite common in autism:

- synaesthesia
- prosopagnosia
- central auditory processing disorder
- Scotopic Sensitivity Syndrome
- sensory integration dysfunction/disorder.

Synaesthesia

Synaesthesia (Greek *syn* – 'together' and *aesthesis* – 'perception') or 'joint sensation' or 'cross-sensory perception' is an involuntary physical experience of a cross-modal association, i.e. the stimulation of one sensory modality triggers a perception in one or more different senses.

Synaesthesia can be of two types:

1. Two-sensory synaesthesia, when stimulation of one modality triggers the perception in a second modality, in the absence of direct stimulation of this second modality. The examples of this type are:

    - coloured-hearing or chromaesthesia: when a sound triggers the perception of a colour

- coloured-olfaction: when a smell triggers the perception of a colour

- coloured-tactility: when a touch triggers a colour

- coloured-gustation: when a taste triggers the perception of a colour

- tactile-hearing: when a sound triggers tactile sensation

- tactile-vision: when a sight triggers feeling shapes and textures pressing the skin

- tactile-gustation: when a taste is experienced as a shape

- audiomotor: when the sounds of different words trigger different postures or movements of the body etc.

2.   Multiple sensory synaesthesia:

  - coloured-numbers: when numbers are heard or read they are experienced as colours

  - coloured-letters: when letters are heard or read they are experienced as colours

  - coloured-graphemes: when words are heard or read they are experienced as colours

  - shaped-numbers: when numbers are heard or read they are experienced as shapes, etc.

In synaesthesia there can be thirty possibilities of different combinations of senses, but usually two senses are involved. Some synaesthetes smell sights or taste shapes, others see sounds. Practically every combination has been reported.

More often synaesthesia is unidirectional, i.e. for example, sight may be experienced as touch but touch does not trigger visual perceptions.

One in every 25,000 people is reported to have synaesthesia (Cytowic 1989), but this estimate might be far too low. Simon Baron-Cohen (1996), an experimental psychologist at Cambridge University, suggests that perhaps one in 2000 people is synaesthetic. Women synaesthetes predominate: a ratio is reported from 3:1 (Cytowic 1989) to 8:1

(Baron-Cohen *et al.* 1993). Synaesthesia appears more frequently among left-handed people and is believed to be genetic. Fifteen per cent of people with synaesthesia are reported to have a history of one of their first-degree relatives having dyslexia, autism or ADD (Cytowic 1995). Synaesthetic experience is very individual, for example, among people who see coloured sounds there is no specific colour for each sound from person to person. Learning disabilities seem more common in synaesthetes, however, the actual incidence of autism among synaesthetes is not known at present.

Cytowic (1995) defines the following five diagnostic features of synaesthesia:

1. Synaesthesia is involuntary. It is a passive experience that happens to someone. The sensations cannot be suppressed or incurred, though the intensity is influenced by the situation they occur in.

2. Synaesthesia is projected into the environment: it is not just in the head but the individual actually sees a sound, hears a sight, etc.; it is perceived externally in peri-personal space, the limb-axis space immediately surrounding the body.

3. Synaesthetic perceptions are durable and generic, i.e. they do not change over time or situation and they are always experienced with the stimulus.

4. Synaesthesia is memorable: the synaesthetic sensations are remembered best.

5. Synaesthesia is emotional: having this experience causes ecstasy.

One of the most common features of synaesthetes is their superior memory (due to their parallel sensations). They remember conversations, verbal instructions and spatial location of objects in every detail. They usually perform in the superior range of the Wechsler Memory Scale (Cytowic 1995). Synaesthetes often remember the secondary perception better than the primary one. A typical complaint is 'I can't remember his name, but I know it's purple' (Lemley 1999). The most famous Russian synaesthete, referred to as S., described by Luria in his book *The Mind of a Mnemonist* (1987), accounts for his ability to remember words:

...I recognize a word not only by the images it evokes but by a whole complex of feelings that image arouses. It's hard to express...it's not a matter of vision or hearing but some over-all sense I get. Usually I experience a word's taste and weight, and I don't have to make an effort to remember it – the word seems to remember itself.

However, this phenomenal experience, though very useful in remembering things, could lead to complications. S.'s understanding of spoken or written speech was literal. Each word evoked images that distracted him from the meaning of the sentence as a whole. He could only understand what he could visualize (Luria 1987).

Synaesthetes are observed to have uneven cognitive skills. They are reported to prefer order, neatness, symmetry and balance. They are more prone to unusual experiences such as déjà vu, clairvoyance, etc. (Cytowic 1995). Among their deficiencies the most commonly reported are right-left confusion (allochiria), poor math skills and a poor sense of direction. Here we can see some similarity between the synaesthetic and autistic features. In some autistic individuals their resistance to changes, insistence on order and routine, echolalia (triggered by some stimuli), an exceptional memory for details, a poor sense of direction, etc. might be caused by synaesthesia.

There are several theories concerning the origin of synaesthesia. The most recent one is the Neonatal Synaesthesia (NS) hypothesis proposed by Maurer (1993). The author states that all human babies (neonates) have synaesthesia, i.e. experience undifferentiated sensory input, probably up to about four–six months of age. This hypothesis refutes Piaget's developmental theory that the different sensory systems are independent at birth and only gradually become integrated with one another. Maurer's hypothesis needs more evidence to be proven, however, there are some indirect data that support his idea, for example, neonates of other species (kittens, hamsters, etc.) have similar transient connections between visual, auditory, somatosensory and motorcortex (Dehay, Bullier and Kennedy 1984). Maurer (1993) suggests the same could be true of human babies. Some autistic people also believe that synaesthesia is an earlier phase of sensory systems development: it 'comes from a time before fixed sensory integration, before taste was taste and smell was smell, sound was sound, touch was touch and vision was vision' (Williams 1998, p.127).

If, according to the NS theory, synaesthesia is a normal phase of development, then adult synaesthesia, as was suggested by Baron-Cohen *et al.* (1993), might represent a breakdown in the process of modularization. Thus, following an early initial phase of normal synaesthesia, a different (adult-like) pattern of the differentiation of the perceptual system is developed because of the development of more rapid and efficient information processing and adult synaesthesia, therefore, represents a failure to develop differentiation of the senses.

We can draw a parallel. In autism there are some phases of development that do not follow a common path. For example, infantile reflexes that are meant to become inhibited naturally in early infancy through feedback to the brain regarding changes in growth and adaptations to the environment, sometimes fail to be replaced by more functional ones and are still present in autistic adults (Williams 1996). Probably, synaesthesia in autism is another 'remnant' that fails to become inhibited.

Most people with synaesthesia do not complain of their condition because for them it is their normal perception of the world and they are not aware of it causing any disadvantages. Moreover, they often enjoy it and think that losing their unique perception would be upsetting, 'just like losing one of your senses' (Duffy cited in Lemley 1999). This leads to the paradoxical conclusion that dysmodularity is not always maladaptive (Baron-Cohen 1996). Though it is true only if synaesthesia is unidirectional, whereas in case of 'two-ways' synaesthesia (when, for example, a synaesthete not only sees colours when he hears sounds, but also hears sounds whenever he sees colours) the individual really suffers from the condition. Baron-Cohen (1996) enumerates possible ill-effects of this type of synaesthesia: stress, dizziness, information overload, avoidance of noisy or colourful places, that lead to social withdrawal and interference with ordinary life.

Sometimes synaesthetic experiences can hinder understanding of the situation. For example, S. reported: 'If, say, a person says something I see the word; but should another person's voice break in, blurs appear. These creep into the syllables of the words and I can't make out what is being said' (Luria 1987).

Though the fact that synaesthesia does occur in autism is recognized, it is considered to be rare (Cesaroni and Garber 1991). Probably, the reported low incidence of synaesthesia in autism can be accounted for by the fact that it is not easily detected in the autistic population. There are several reasons for this:

- Communication problems: even verbal individuals have difficulties in expressing their experiences.

- Even non-autistic synaesthetes find it difficult to realize that they experience the world differently and it might be hard for them to imagine that others cannot, say, hear sounds while seeing colours. It is we who must find out whether they experience synaesthesia.

The analysis of the personal accounts of autistic individuals shows that synaesthesia is not rare in this population and practically all combinations of senses have been found. Such senses as sight, sound and touch are involved more often than smell and taste. Below are descriptions of experiences that can be defined as synaesthetic.

Tactile-hearing

I loved the way most words play on my tongue…[some words] hurt my ears. (Willey 1999, p.20)

…words that tickled, words that warmed when I spoke them…(some voices, especially with heavy nasal or high shrill qualities, or extreme eastern or southern accents) sting my ears like a wet towel slapped against my eardrum would. (Willey 1999, p.31)

Tactile-visual

I would refuse words that looked ugly by virtue of being too lopsided or too cumbersome or too unusual in their phonetics. (Willey 1999, p.20)

I knew I had written something great when I found words that looked, sounded or felt good. (Willey 1999, p.31)

Olfactory-visual

> It is possible…not only to see colours, but almost to smell them, too. (O'Neill 1999, p.29)

Gustatory-olfactory

> [As a reaction to the perfume] my mouth tasted like I had eaten a bunch of sickly smelling flowers. (Williams 1999, p.57)

One individual with autism (cited in Cesaroni and Garber 1991) describes the experience of sounds as 'vague sensations of colour, shape, texture, movement, scent or flavour. It is as if information was received in several modes even though the signal comes from one source.' Jim Sinclair (1998) speaks about the colours of voices and the tactility of music. Donna Williams (1996) experiences some people ('fluffy people') 'causing her lemons' because 'it triggers a sensation that feels exactly how eating lemons' makes her feel:

> Though the taste isn't there, the response in my mouth and neck and muscles is the same. These people cause a 'sour taste' that is as extreme and of the same type that lemons cause me when eaten. (Williams 1996, p. 90)

What to look for:

Vision:

1. Covers/rubs/hits/blinks eyes in response to a sound/taste/smell/touch

2. Complains about (is frustrated with) the 'wrong' colours of letters/numbers, etc. written on coloured blocks, etc.

Hearing:

1. Covers/hits ears in response to a visual stimulus/taste/smell/touch/texture

2. Complains about (is frustrated with) a sound in response to colours/textures/scent/flavour/touch

Taste:

1. Makes swallow movements in response to a visual/auditory stimulus/smell/touch

2. Complains about (is frustrated with) taste in response to a visual/auditory stimulus/smell touch

Smell:

Covers/rubs/hits, etc. the nose in response to a visual/auditory stimulus/taste/touch

Tactility:

1. Complains about (is frustrated with) feeling colours/sounds, etc. while being touched

2. Complains about (is frustrated with) feeling being touched when being looked at

3. Complains about (is frustrated with) backache, etc./heat/cold in colourful/crowded, etc. places with lots of movement

Proprioception/Vestibular:

Involuntary movements/postures of the body in response to a visual/ auditory stimulus/smell/taste

Helen and Alex seem to 'see' sounds. Alex even tries to describe this experience: 'I was scared. I saw a yellow "z-z-z" sound', 'The eyes saw the wrong word' (in response to a verbal instruction). When Alex is in a state of sensory overload his synaesthetic experiences aggravate his condition and can lead to 'panic attacks' and aggression. After one of these 'incidents' Alex tried to give his explanations of what had happened: 'In the shop I heard black then the word broke down into pieces and they entered my eyes. I became blind because everything was black.'

John displays involuntary movements of the body in response to some auditory stimuli (vacuum cleaners, lawn mowers).

Prosopagnosia ('face-blindness')

Some autistic people are reported to be prosopagnostic (Blackburn 1999; Grandin 1996a), i.e. they have trouble recognizing people's faces. This condition makes them blind to all but the most familiar faces. Prosopagnosia may be genetic and runs in families, or may be caused by strokes, head injuries or severe illnesses. Face-blindness may co-occur with autistic spectrum disorders. Hans Asperger reported the example of an astronomer with Asperger syndrome who could not recognize his friends and relatives. Some researchers (Kracke 1994) even suggest that prosopagnosia may be an essential symptom in autistic spectrum disorder, perhaps a specific subgroup of Asperger syndrome.

The exact effects and severity may vary between people. Temple Grandin (1996a), for example, often got into embarrassing situations because she did not remember faces unless she had seen the people many times or they had a very distinct facial feature, such as a big beard, thick glasses or a strange hairstyle.

Some experimental studies of autistic people's capacity to process faces suggest that they use abnormal processing strategies and experience less difficulties when faces are presented to them upside-down. Whether it is true for their perception of the whole environment needs further investigation.

Non-autistic prosopagnostics state that face-blindness tends to isolate them from people in general, as being unable to recognize others interferes with making and maintaining relationships (Bill 1997). They work out their own recognition system. Most common features that seem to work best for face-blind people are casual clothes, long hair and facial hair, and movement. Bill, who is face-blind, describes his method of recognizing people by their jeans, gait, movements and hair (as the inability to recognize faces does not extend to hair, particularly if it is long enough to extend out of the face area). He can see a pattern in hair texture and process hairlines. Interestingly, many autistic people are reported to be fascinated by people's hair, and many do not recognize their relatives if they wear unfamiliar clothes. A prosopagnostic autistic boy, despite knowing the names of his classmates, more often calls them 'a boy' or 'a girl'. Interestingly, when one of the girls had her hair cut short, he 'moved' her to the 'boy' category.

Another problem prosopagnostic people experience is difficulty in understanding and expressing emotions. The main 'tools' to express emotions are not words but facial expressions, gestures and tone of voice. For people who cannot 'read' faces because of face-blindness or cannot 'hear' emotions in voices because of their central auditory processing disorder (see below) it is extremely difficult not only to understand emotions in others but also to express emotions themselves otherwise than using words. Bill (1997) calls it 'emotion blindness'. Being prosopagnostic Bill was struck by the similarity of emotional expressions of blind people and prosopagnostics. He assumes that not seeing what emotions are supposed to look like when coming in, both the blind and prosopagnostics never acquired a large repertoire of emotions to send out. It is no wonder, therefore, that autistic people experiencing all sorts of sensory processing problems find it most difficult to understand the emotional states of other people and their own.

In addition to their difficulties in 'reading' facial expressions, some prosopagnostic people have problems with understanding gestures and sign language, which involves a lot of facial expression (Bill 1997).

Central auditory processing disorder (CAPD)

Autism is often associated with auditory processing disorders (problems). Auditory problems in autism investigated in the literature include hypersensitivity (Delacato 1974; Grandin 1996a, b; 1999; Grandin and Scariano 1986); hyposensitivity/unresponsiveness to certain sounds (Kanner 1943; Koegel and Schreibman 1976); inability to modulate certain sounds (Ornitz 1974); delays in auditory processing (Condon 1975; Rimland 1964) and others. These problems may be covered by a single definition – auditory dysfunction.

This dysfunction is often undetected, as a conventional hearing test may not show any problems, especially in older children and adults who have acquired strategies to cope with their difficulties, such as blocking out sounds.

Recently a subtype of auditory dysfunction has been singled out and described as central auditory processing disorder (CAPD). CAPD is defined as a neurological dysfunction responsible for impairments of neural pathways of the brain that link the ear with the central auditory system when the ear works properly but the parts of the brain that interpret and analyse the auditory information do not. The child can hear but has problems with listening. The causes of CAPD are unknown.

French otolaryngologist and psychologist A. A. Tomatis has developed Audio-Psycho-Phonology as a multi-disciplinary science (hearing, speech/language development and psychological attitudes) and the Tomatis Method to affect speech, language, learning and social interaction. Dr Tomatis conducted research in the ability to hear in two groups of people: factory workers in war plants daily subjected to auditory overload, and professional opera singers who had lost the ability to sing. Paradoxically, audiometric testing showed that both groups displayed similar patterns: hearing loss in the same frequencies. Tomatis formulated his theory – the Tomatis Effect – 'a person can only reproduce vocally what he is capable of hearing', i.e. auditory and vocal organs are part of the same neurological loop and changes in the auditory system will immediately bring changes in the voice, and vice versa. Tomatis hypothesized that the ear can be 'retuned' to hearing faulty frequencies and that, in turn, can alter one's self-listening and production of sounds. Tomatis developed the Tomatis Method to use sound stimulation in order to provide corrective auditory opportunities.

Tomatis distinguished between hearing (the ability to perceive the sound) and listening (the ability to filter irrelevant sounds and focus on sounds we are listening). According to Tomatis, listening problems (if they are not physiological) are psychological. Listening abilities are vital for the development of communication. The researcher thought that psychological problems such as difficult birth, disruptive home environment, physical and emotional abuse could cause shutting out auditory stimuli and thus, create a relaxation of the muscles of the middle ear. If the muscles of the ear are inactive for too long, they lose their tonicity. As a result, the sounds are distorted and incorrectly analysed (Tomatis 1991).

Tomatis worked out the Tomatis Listening Test aimed to find out the person's level of good listening criteria:

- hearing within normal range

- absence of auditory distortions

- the ability to analyse and compare sounds of different frequencies ('auditory selectivity')

- the ability to identify the source of the sound; a right-sided auditory dominance, etc.

The failure of one or several of these characteristics results in impaired listening. Tomatis developed special techniques to restore 'good listening', i.e. functional effectiveness of the ear. (See the Tomatis Method in Chapter 7 below.)

Guy Berard, a French otolaryngologist, originally trained by Tomatis, disagreed with his teacher on a number of points and developed his own approach to the problem. In contrast to Tomatis, who assumed psychological causes of the disorder, Berard suggested biological causes. According to Dr Berard, processing problems may occur if a person hears some frequencies better than the others and develops 'auditory peaks' (frequencies to which a person is hypersensitive).

Some indicators of CAPD (from different sources) are:

- may seem deaf at some occasions but hears the slightest sounds at other occasions

- covers ears even if there are no loud sounds (seems to hear sounds which other people do not hear)

- a very light sleeper

- produces sounds (banging doors, tapping things, making vocalizations, etc.)

- cannot concentrate in noisy environments

- speech problems.

Scotopic Sensitivity/Irlen Syndrome (SS/IS)

The idea that vision must have something to do with difficulty in reading and spelling has been highlighted from the earliest times. The first neurologist who investigated this problem was Samuel Orton. He called this phenomenon 'strephosymbolia' (i.e. 'twisted symbols'), applying it to people without identified visual impairments who, nevertheless, saw a printed text in a distorted way (Orton 1928).

In the 1970s–1980s the idea that visual perception might influence the reading performance was investigated again. The visual perception of dyslexics was stated to be different from that of normal readers (Jordan 1972). Distortions of print when reading were reported by Meares (1980). The researchers found out that visual acuity did not necessarily correlate with reading performance. In the following decades there have appeared some studies that identified particular types of visual abnormalities as possible factors in reading difficulties. Wilkins (1995) investigated the effects of visual stimuli on epilepsy. The researcher suggested that fluorescent lights and certain patterns (especially stripes) might cause problems for people with epilepsy.

In 1983, perceptual problems caused by light sensitivity were identified by Helen Irlen, an educational psychologist, who worked with adults with dyslexia. She discovered that a visual perceptual dysfunction, unrelated to visual skills normally assessed by ophthalmic examination, may cause distortions with print and environment. Helen Irlen suggests that there are people whose problem is not in the processing of information but in the inability to get it through one of the channels, namely vision. She states that these individuals are highly sensitive to particular wavelengths and frequencies of the white light spectrum leading to rapid fatigue after only short periods of reading, thus giving rise to a reading disability, headaches and stress. Irlen called the cluster of symptoms of this dysfunction Scotopic Sensitivity Syndrome (now known as Scotopic Sensitivity/Irlen Syndrome – SS/IS). SS/IS is a visual-perceptual problem that occurs in some people with learning/reading disorders, autism, and other developmental disorders. The symptoms include (Irlen 1989; 1991; 1997):

1. Light sensitivity: difficulty concentrating or discomfort in fluorescent lighting, bright sunlight, glare or lights at night.

2. Contrast and colour sensitivity: problems with high contrast such as black on white, bright colours and busy patterns such as stripes and polka dots.

3.   Poor print resolution: difficulty reading print, numbers or musical notes. Problems may include print that shifts, shakes, blurs, moves, doubles, swirls, sparkles, shimmers or disappears.

4.   Restricted span of recognition: inability to read letters, numbers, musical notes or words in groups, or to see objects in the environment together. This results in problems tracking, correctly identifying words, or the ability to skim or speed read.

5.   Attention deficit: problems concentrating while doing tasks such as reading, writing, computer use, looking and even listening.

6.   Poor depth perception: inability to judge distances or spatial relationships affecting small and gross motor coordination. May be unsure or have difficulty with such things as escalators, stairs, ball sports or driving.

7.   Strain and fatigue: physical symptoms are varied and include, but are not limited to, fatigue, tiredness, headaches, fidgetiness, distractibility and hyperactivity.

Irlen (1991) identified a variety of ways in which a printed page might be perceived by a person with SS/IS, such as the rivers effect, the washout effect, the swirl effect, the blurry effect, the halo effect, etc.

The symptoms described by Irlen were not identified in the previous investigations because questions were not asked about how reading disabled people see the print. It has appeared that they are usually not aware that what they are seeing is abnormal (Irlen 1991; Jordan 1972). Optical professionals failed to identify this dysfunction as they had never directed their questioning to how a child sees print (Meares 1980). A number of probable causal mechanisms have been suggested: the transient system deficit, magnocellular/central processing deficit theory, the retinal sensitivity theory, the biochemical anomalies theory (for a review see Robinson 1998).

Originally, SS/IS was considered a visual-spatial subtype of reading disability. Recent research (Riley 1999) has shown that SS/IS (in a milder degree) affects about 20 per cent of the general population as well. They experience difficulties with a normal working environment, particularly fluorescent lighting and computer screens, resulting in fatigue, eyestrain, headaches, poor concentration, inefficiency and stress. SS/IS can be associated with other disorders. Most research has been devoted to SS/IS in people with dyslexia. However, in the 1990s there arose an interest in SS/IS in autism.

In 1993 Donna Williams and her husband were screened for SS/IS and got the Irlen lenses. Although Donna was aware of the fact that she saw differently from other people, for the first time was she able to experience how great this difference was: for the first time she could *see* other people's faces and the world around her clearly and as a whole (Williams 1999).

It was these changes in the visual perception of individuals with autism by means of the coloured lenses that highlighted new perspectives in the research of SS/IS. After several years experience of working with autistic individuals Helen Irlen has come to the conclusion that though the symptoms displayed by people with autism are not any different from those of individuals with learning and reading problems, autistic people experience more severe perceptual difficulties. The sensory overload caused by bright lights, fluorescent lights, colours and patterns makes the body react as if it is being attacked or bombarded, resulting in negative biochemical changes. This may result in such physical symptoms as headaches, anxiety, panic attacks or aggression. In order to lessen the stress caused by 'sensory bombardment', individuals use their 'defensive visual behaviours' – looking away, looking in short glances, looking through fingers, looking down, or shut down their visual channel altogether.

Sensory integration dysfunction

About 10 per cent of people are estimated to have sensory integration dysfunction. Sensory integrative problems are found in up to 70 per cent of children with learning difficulties. Sensory integrative difficulties have been identified in people with autism and other developmental disabilities. But what exactly is sensory integration dysfunction?

The theory of sensory integration dysfunction (SID) was formulated by A. Jane Ayres (1979), an occupational therapist, to describe a *variety* of neurological disorders. It attempts to account for the relationship between sensory processing and behavioural deficits, and is known as a 'theory of brain-behaviour relationships' (Fisher and Murray 1991). At present SID still remains a theory and has little recognition and support from the fields outside occupational therapy (OT). There is still much scepticism and criticism of SID. Below we will try to answer the 'why is it so' question and see whether scepticism is justifiable or not. There seem to be several reasons to account for the criticism received by the theory of SID.

To start with, the choice of the term 'sensory integration dysfunction/ disorder' was very unfortunate. On the one hand, SID allows a very broad interpretation as it was introduced to cover a variety of neurological disorders. On the other hand, it effectively narrows the investigation, as it excludes any other disorder labelled by a different term, for example, sensory processing disorders. As a result, despite the theory having been actively developed within the field of OT, it has inevitably ignored a great amount of research in the field of sensory and information processing as being outside the scope of OT interests. It is no wonder, therefore, to find such statements as 'the state of knowledge regarding modulation of sensation was in its infancy during the 1980s' in a review of OT literature (Wilbarger and Stackhouse 1998). On the contrary, quite a lot of research was being carried out in the field of sensory dysfunction, including sensory modulation problems, in the 1960s–80s.

In the 1960s, Bernard Rimland (1964) wrote about impairments in perceptual abilities of autistic children. Edward Ornitz (1969) described disorders of perception in autism. In the early 1970s, Carl Delacato (1974) put forward the theory of sensory dysfunction in autism, and proposed a classification of abnormal sensory experiences of autistic children. Delacato also pioneered the treatment of sensory abnormalities by 'normalizing' sensory processing. Though his book was published more than three decades ago, his basic ideas about sensory dysfunction are still relevant today. Actually, these ideas have 're-appeared' in many works of OT research in the 1980s–90s as 'new discoveries'.

In 1989, Ornitz extended the notion of a disorder of sensory processing to the notion of disorders of sensory and information processing. This approach allowed him to clarify and identify separate stages and functions of sensory perception and consider information processing in terms of more discrete functions, such as attention, memory and learning.

Another drawback of the SID theory was that it was presented to describe a new phenomenon that had not been investigated before. Consequently, it ignored much of the previous research in the field of sensory processing, and limited itself to the field of OT.

It is important to remember that the SID theory was not new, but its name was. Before SID, the same concepts were described under the names of 'sensory perceptual impairments', 'sensory processing disorders/ problems', 'sensory dysfunction', 'disturbances of sensory modulation/ information processing', etc. Even now, after several decades of intensive research in the field of OT, there is great confusion about definitions, concepts and notions related to SI and SID.

In the OT literature I have been unable to find a single, commonly accepted definition of SI(D). Different people either use different terminology to discuss identical phenomenon, or apply one and the same term to cover different meanings, depending on the views, expertise and research interests of the person who uses it. Current works are based on the writings of A. Jane Ayres but the concepts of the theory have been further developed by OT researchers.

In order to trace the development of the concept and define the current understanding of SI(D), we shall briefly discuss the definitions presented in the OT literature. They can be roughly divided into broad and narrow.

The broad definitions

Ayres (1989) defined SI as 'the neurological process that organizes sensation from one's own body and from the environment and makes it possible to use the body effectively within the environment. The spatial and temporal aspects of inputs from different sensory modalities are interpreted, associated and united' (Ayres 1989, p.11). In accordance with this broad definition, some authors describe SI as the process by which the nervous system receives, organizes, files and integrates sensory information in order to make an appropriate response (Herron 1993); the ability to take in information through senses, to put it together with prior information, memories, and knowledge stored in the brain, and to make a meaningful response (Stephens 1997).

And now let us compare these definitions with those of perception and sensory processing: perception is the process by which an organism collects, interprets and comprehends information from the outside world by means of senses. Sensory processing is the ability of the brain to process all sensations so we can interact adequately with our environment.

Confusing? You bet!

This broad interpretation of SI leads to broad interpretation of SID, such as the ineffective neurological processing of information received through the senses. (Though some occupational therapists do distinguish between sensory processing dysfunction and SID, where sensory processing is the way the body takes in 'raw data' of sensations from the environment through all of the sense organs, and sensory integration refers to the way the brain combines and utilizes that raw information in order to provide useful information with which we can make a decision.)

The narrow definitions

Below are just few examples of narrower interpretations of SI(D). SI is distinguishing between sensory experiences, such as touch, movement, body awareness, sight, sound, smell, taste and the pull of gravity (Kapes 2001). SID is a disruption in the process of intake, organization and output of sensory information. Inefficient sensory intake is taking in too much or too little information. With too much information, the brain is on overload and causes an individual to avoid sensory stimuli. With too little information, the brain seeks more sensory stimuli (Kranowitz 1998, p.55). This latter explanation coincides completely with Delacato's classification of hyper- and hyposensitivities (however, Delacato distinguished a third possibility – 'white noise', as well).

In a narrow sense, SID is nowadays often used interchangeably with sensory modulation disorder/disruption. This brings even more confusion, as this 'interchange' is not accepted by all the researchers, and some authors interpret 'modulation' as a separate process.

Similarly, we find broad and narrow meanings of 'modulation' in the OT literature. Ayres defined modulation as the 'brain's regulation of its own activity' (1979, p.182), and placed the role of vestibular system in a key position in modulation.

Other examples of the understanding of the notion of sensory modulation and sensory modulation disorder/problems include the following ideas.

Sensory modulation is 'a tendency to generate responses that are appropriately graded in relation to incoming sensory stimuli rather than underreacting or overreacting to them' (Parham and Mailloux 1996). Modulation is the critical balance or regulation of facilitating and inhibiting effects (Myles *et al.* 2001). 'When an individual overresponds, underresponds or fluctuates in response to sensory input in a manner disproportional to that input, we say that the individual has a sensory modulation disorder' (Koomar and Bundy 1991, p.268). Wilbarger and Stackhouse (1998), having failed to discover a satisfying definition of sensory modulation, propose their own conceptualization of it: sensory modulation is the intake of sensation via typical sensory processing mechanisms so that the degree, intensity and quality of response is graded to match environmental demand and so that a range of optimal performance/adaptation is maintained. In their review of OT literature on sensory modulation they regret that there is limited information written about sensory modulation, and emphasize the necessity to update 'our theories to incorporate the new findings in order to facilitate acceptance of our unique perspective on central nervous system functioning as it relates to human occupation'. One should add, it is equally important to incorporate the 'old findings' from the outside of OT, such as, for example, those described by Ornitz (1983; 1985; 1989) – the disturbances of sensory modulation manifested as both underreactivity and overreactivity to sensory stimuli.

As we will see further, all these different interpretations of SID allow for highlighting different characteristics and categories. As any aspect of sensory processing and information processing can be covered by the term of SID, it gives a researcher a free hand to choose whatever they want to study, describing it as SID. Stephens (1997), for instance, discusses various characteristics of SID under four categories: attention and regularity problems, sensory defensiveness, activity patterns and behaviour. Herron (1993) includes in the end products of SI such characteristics as the ability to register and modulate stimuli, motor coordination, attention, motor planning ability, balance, eye control, emotional stability, behavioural control, body scheme and self-esteem. Kranowitz, the author of *The Out-of-Sync Child: Recognizing and Coping with Sensory Integration Dysfunction* (1998) describes modulation, inhibition, habituation and facilitation. Myles and colleagues distinguish five stages of the SI process: registration, orientation, interpretation, organization and execution of a response. They also suggest that sensory modulation (not included by them in the five stages of the SI process) supports the effective performance by further integrating the information to result in a behaviour or action that matches our intent (Myles *et al.* 2001, p.13). Still others enumerate such 'common sensory-processing problems' as registration, modulation, defensiveness and integration.

Originally, Ayres limited her investigation with three senses – tactile, vestibular, and proprioceptive – defined as the basic ones. Later OT researchers included all the senses in the theory.

Ayres introduced the concepts of tactile defensiveness (for tactile sense), gravitational insecurity (vestibular system) and postural insecurity (proprioception). She defined tactile defensiveness as avoiding or negative reactions to non-noxious tactile stimuli (Ayres 1964) and as an imbalance between discriminative and protective sensory processing. Tactile defensiveness is manifested in 'fright, flight, or fight' response or reaction. However, the concept of defensiveness in the context of SID seems to be misleading as it implies the reaction (i.e. the behaviour caused by something) rather than the cause of this reaction.

This concept has been expanded and developed into a broader category by numerous OT researchers and placed on all sorts of continua. To name just a few:

- sensory defensiveness (= an imbalance of inhibitory and excitatory forces) as opposed to sensory dormancy ('too much...inhibition of incoming sensory stimuli' (Knickerbocker 1980, p.32))

- tactile defensiveness – registration problems continuum (Fisher and Dunn 1983)

- sensory defensiveness and sensory dormancy (as sensory modulation disorders) as opposing ends of a sensory responsivity/registration continuum with overorientation at one end and a failure to orient on the other (Royeen 1989)

- sensory defensiveness on a continuum of approach and avoidance behaviours (Wilbarger and Wilbarger 1991)

- registration problems – sensory defensiveness (Parham and Mailloux 1996).

Gradually, the shift from sensory defensiveness to sensory modulation problems (a person's threshold for sensory events and responsiveness to sensation) was made. It seems quite logical, as hypersensitivity (overarousal, overreactivity) experienced by the individual causes defensiveness (reaction/behaviour). This turn of attention from behaviours to experiences probably prevented such terms as 'visual defensiveness'/'auditory defensiveness'/'vestibular defensiveness', etc. from being spread in the research literature. That is why, though OT researchers still write about tactile defensiveness, while describing problems in other sensory modalities they prefer to use 'hyper-/hyposensitivities', 'registration/modulation/integration' problems, i.e. the concepts of sensory dysfunction and sensory modulation disturbances introduced by the researchers in the field of sensory and information processing.

The better prognosis for children 'who register sensory input but failed to modulate it' than for children who fail to register sensory input, suggested by Ayres and Tickle (1980, p.375) also coincides completely with the prognosis by Delacato (1974) for children with hypersensitivities as opposed to those with hyposensitivities.

Common classifications of 'original' SIDs include:

- *Decreased discrimination of vestibular and proprioceptive information*: poor posture, frequent falling, clumsiness, poor balance, constant moving and fidgeting, poor attention. Treatment generally focuses on providing intense vestibular and proprioceptive stimulation and improving postural responses (Koomar and Bundy 1991).

- *Decreased discrimination of tactile information*: a poor body scheme, difficulty with praxis and poor hand skill development.

Treatment generally focuses on providing a variety of deep- and light-touch experiences (Koomar and Bundy 1991).

- *Somatodyspraxia*: poor tactile and proprioceptive processing, clumsiness, frequent tripping, falling and bumping into objects, difficulty with motor and manipulation skills, poor organization (Cermak 1991).

- *Impaired bilateral motor coordination*: difficulty with bilateral activities such as clapping, hopping, skipping, keyboarding; difficulty developing a hand preference. Treatment generally focuses on providing vestibular and proprioceptive experiences and graded bilateral activities (Koomar and Bundy 1991).

- *Tactile defensiveness*: an aversive response to a variety of tactile experiences.

- *Gravitational insecurity*: limited participation in gross motor play; avoidance or fear of escalators, elevators, cars or planes; resistance of being off the ground. Treatment focuses on providing proprioceptive input and graded vestibular input (Koomar and Bundy 1991).

- *Projected action sequences*: inability to plan and initiate movement in response to changing environmental stimuli. These difficulties are thought to be connected with inefficiencies in processing vestibular and proprioceptive input (Koomar and Bundy 1991).

Nowadays, the OT researchers extend SID to the problems in all senses. According to Sensory Integration International, the following are some signs of SID:

- oversensitivity to touch, movement, sights, or sounds

- underreactivity to touch, movement, sights, or sounds

- tendency to be easily distracted

- social and/or emotional problems

- activity level that is unusually high or unusually low

- physical clumsiness or apparent carelessness

- impulsive, lacking in self-control
- difficulty making transitions from one situation to another
- inability to unwind or calm self
- poor self concept
- delays in speech, language, or motor skills
- delays in academic achievement.

These signs are often complemented by more specific symptoms from all sensory modalities and often coincide with the symptoms of CAPD or SS/IS described above.

At present there are two distinct views on the 'status' of SID. Some authors argue that numerous psychological, psychiatric and neurological disorders such as schizophrenia, depression, ADHD, ADD, autism, PDD, Tourette syndrome, etc. appear the same as SID, and that many symptoms of SID look like symptoms of other common disabilities, making it difficult to differentiate one difficulty from another (Nelson undated). The others (Wilbarger and Stackhouse 1998) think that referring to the cluster of SI problems as a disorder may be premature as SID has not been identified as having universal and persistent features that are distinct from other established disorders.

One can make some suggestions. Instead of trying to embrace all sensory processing and information processing disorders under one umbrella term, wouldn't it better to investigate specific patterns of sensory perceptual problems in different 'established disorders'? For example, though sensory perceptual problems have not been incorporated into diagnostic classifications, very specific and easy-to-describe unusual responses to sensory stimuli have been reported in most autistic children when they are observed prior to six years of age or when their parents are questioned about specific behaviours (Ornitz 1969; 1974; 1983; 1985). Before the age of six, specific behaviours caused by sensory perceptual problems were observed with almost the same frequencies as behaviours related to social and communicative impairments (Ornitz, Guthrie and Farley 1977; 1978; Volkmar, Cohen and Paul 1986). It would be useful to compile specific patterns of sensory perceptual problems for different developmental disorders in order to find out whether there are differences in their manifestations.

To make the process easier, one could clearly specify and define separate sensory processing and information processing phenomena. For instance, sensory integration dysfunction can be defined as difficulty processing and interpreting information from more than one sensory channel at a time; sensory modulation disturbances – the difficulties to modulate optimal arousal, that is manifested as both under- and overreactivity (hyper- and hyposensitivities) to sensory stimuli, or fluctuation between the two; etc.

Then probably SID, sensory modulation problems, as well as CAPD, SS/IS and similar conditions, will fit perfectly into the theory of sensory perceptual disorders/problems/difficulties.

Chapter 7

Treatments

When a child is diagnosed autistic, educational priorities focus on behavioural interventions aimed at development of social and communicative skills, while the child's 'sensory needs' are often ignored. Paradoxical as it may seem, sometimes autistic children benefit from being misdiagnosed as having visual and/or auditory impairments. It especially applies to the so-called low-functioning (or 'severely autistic') children whose sensory perceptual problems are usually very severe. Being placed in an environment where their sensory difficulties are addressed these children might respond to social and communication interventions better than if they were placed in autistic units/schools where the main emphasis is only on training in social/communicative behaviours.

In the case of such disabilities as blindness/deafness the main emphasis is on providing sensory substitution in order to replace one sensory input the person lacks (vision/hearing) by another (for example, tactile aids: Braille alphabet) and adjusting the environment to facilitate functioning of people with visual/auditory impairments. The problem with autism specific sensory perceptual difficulties is that they are often 'invisible' and undetected. The first step to make in the direction of addressing these problems is to recognize that they do exist. The matter is complicated by the fact that autistic individuals are very different in their sensory perceptual profile. Treatment programmes that are appropriate and beneficial for one child may be painful and harmful for another. Thus, if the 'right problem' is addressed, the child gets more chances to benefit from the treatment. A widely known example of this is described by Annabel Stehli (1991) concerning her daughter Georgiana who suffered from extremely acute hearing. After the Auditory Integration Treatment her hypersensitivity to sound diminished and this enabled her to cope with other perceptual problems to such an extent that she is no longer considered autistic.

The sensory perceptual profile of a child could be a starting point for selection of methods and, probably, working out new ones, in order to address the individual needs of each particular child.

Without treatment children learn to compensate, and use systems and methods available to them, such as stereotyped behaviours, self-injury, aggression, tantrums and withdrawal.

There are different treatments available to address sensory problems. These do not offer a 'cure' for autism and do not have 100 per cent success for all who undergo them. In this chapter the basic principles of interventions addressing sensory perceptual problems in autism are discussed.

Auditory Integration Training (AIT)

Auditory Integration Training (AIT) was developed by French otolaryngologist Guy Berard. It is based on the work of Berard's supervisor and colleague Alfred Tomatis but differs from it at some very important points. Both methods – the Tomatis Method and Berard's AIT – are used at present. They have been reported to be beneficial in hypersensitive hearing, dyslexia, ADHD and autism, though there is still some controversy in the reports.

The Tomatis Method

The Tomatis Method works at three levels: functional, emotional and relational.

First, the initial assessment is conducted to evaluate the ability to listen, listening strengths and weaknesses. This assessment consists of a battery of tests, which are administered using electronic equipment. The ability to hear specific sound scale frequencies (from 125 to 8000 Hz) is tested and a curve is derived for each ear (threshold evaluation). The curves are examined in three ranges: bass (125–800 Hz), middle (800–3000 Hz), and treble (3000–8000 Hz). In the normal condition, the curves rise at a specific rate between specific frequencies. Disturbances in the curves can be caused by different problems. Then the ability to recognize pitch differences between frequencies is tested for each ear (selectivity evaluation) by using a sound input of about 45–50 db. This ability should be developed by the time a child is eight–ten years of age. In order to discover problems with orientation within one's environment, the ability to orient spatially is tested (spatialization evaluation). Leading ear evaluation is conducted to determine the dominant ear.

Additional tests include examination of lateral dominance, figure drawing (the tree test, family test, human figure test).

After analysis of the test results and a detailed developmental history, a specific individual listening programme using the Electronic Ear (the apparatus developed by Tomatis in 1953) is implemented. The Electronic Ear consists of four mechanisms: filters, electronic gate, balance control, and bone and air conduction reception. It is used to retrain the ear.

The programme consists of two stages: auditory (i.e. receptive, when the person is trained to develop better listening skills) and audio-vocal (i.e. expressive, when the person is trained to develop a voice of good quality and tone to maintain listening skills). The person listens to the sounds of music and voice through the Electronic Ear. Electronically modulated music is administered through earphones. This 'auditory input' is filtered and modified according to the specific auditory problems of each individual. The Listening Training Programme is aimed to simulate five stages of listening development with special attention to the stages where the person displays difficulties. These five stages are: filtered high frequency listening (prenatal listening); integration of low frequencies (sonic birth); humming (prelanguage); repeating words and phrases (language); reading aloud. The first two phases (prenatal listening and sonic birth) are passive, where the child listens to filtered music (usually Mozart) and their mother's voice while they are engaged in some activity (painting, doing puzzles, talking or even sleeping) for two hours a day. The last three phases are active, where the child has to repeat filtered sounds modified by the Electronic Ear. The whole programme usually lasts for 30 days (2 hours a day).

The Tomatis Method is claimed to be beneficial for a number of 'psychological disorders', including autism.

The Berard method of AIT

The AIT method was developed by Guy Berard, who was originally trained by Alfred Tomatis. The publication of Stehli's book *The Sound of a Miracle, A Child's Triumph over Autism* (1991) brought AIT a great attention and interest. Annabel Stehli described the remarkable results of AIT on her daughter Georgiana who had been diagnosed autistic and spent the first 11 years of her life in special residential schools and institutions. The treatment was so effective for Georgie that she could live independently, graduated from the college with a degree and got married.

AIT is based on two theories:

- Behaviour is a direct result of how well a person hears.

- The hearing mechanism can be retrained. As a result, improved hearing leads to improved behaviour.

The principle of AIT originated from the concept of possibility of cure by mechanical needs. For example, if the movement of a limb is restricted, it can be cured (trained) by special physical exercises to increase mobility. This 'mechanical' treatment influences not only the related muscles but also the related area of the brain. Berard implies this principle in his 'ear training': if one of the areas of the auditory system is stimulated (trained) by certain sound training (with frequencies causing hypersensitivity having been filtered out) hearing is normalized. Research has shown that in order for the nervous system to develop normally, it must receive adequate sensory input that stimulates the development of corresponding areas in the brain.

Berard developed an AIT device – Audiokinetron Ears Education and Retraining System. It selects on random high and low frequencies from music and sends the sounds via headphones.

The AIT procedure involves:

- Audiometric testing to find out whether the person has 'auditory peaks'. According to Berard, these auditory peaks can be reduced or eliminated by AIT.

- The filtering out of sounds at certain selected frequencies in accordance with the individual audiogram. Where an accurate audiogram cannot be obtained, the basic modulation system without specific filters is used.

- The modulation of the music by alternatively dampening and enhancing, on a random basis, the bass and treble musical output. Each session lasts for 30 minutes, 2 sessions a day for 10 days.

- After five days, another assessment of the person's hearing to find out whether the auditory peaks are still present and whether there is a need to readjust the filters. If the person has speech and/or language problems, after half the sessions the volume level for the left ear is reduced to stimulate the language development in the left hemisphere.

After AIT, the person should perceive all the frequencies equally well and have no auditory peaks.

During the treatment and for some time after it some people exhibit temporary behavioural problems, such as hyperactivity, rapid mood swings and even aggression. It seems that the more severe the side-effects, the more beneficial the treatment is for the person. Typically, these behaviours do not last long (from two days to two months). Dr Berard explains AIT and summarizes case histories of some of his patients, with copies of their hearing tests before and after the treatment, in his book *Hearing Equals Behavior* (published in France in 1982; the English translation, 1993).

Numerous pilot studies of the method demonstrated significant results: a reduction in self-stimulatory behaviours, hyperactivity, anxiety, social withdrawal, distractibility and echolalia, and an increase in attention, comprehension, articulation and auditory memory. There are very few immediate changes after the treatment. Usually positive changes take several months to be noticed. Most common positive changes are in the areas of social, emotional and cognitive development. Lower functioning individuals typically show greater improvement. It is not known yet how AIT affects a person's behaviours.

The report on the efficacy of AIT summarizing the results and critiques of 28 studies (January, 1993–May, 2001) was prepared by Edelson and Rimland (2001). The report covers 28 studies of AIT with 23 concluding that AIT benefits various population subgroups, 3 claiming no benefit, and 2 with contradictory results. Dr Rimland considers that the Berard Method is more effective than the Tomatis therapy, which is more likely to produce side-effects, and is more expensive and intrusive. Besides,

Tomatis's emphasis on supposed psychological and/or emotional causes of the disorder can be misleading.

The treatment is used with people with auditory processing problems, including those with autism, dyslexia, learning disabilities, PDD, ADHD and others. However, some researchers feel strongly against the treatment and warn that AIT can be harmful for children as the sound level of the processed music used in AIT might well exceed the maximum allowable levels as specified by the Occupational Safety and Health Administration in the USA.

So why does the treatment work with some children and harm others? As there is no definite answer to this question at present, we may suggest the following hypothesis. We know that many people with autism do suffer from auditory problems (especially hypersensitivity to certain sounds). AIT aims to reduce this hypersensitivity by retraining the ear to tolerate certain frequencies and pitches. However, we should always address the causes of auditory hypersensitivity and not the symptom per se. Very often hypersensitivity is caused not by certain frequencies or certain sounds but by the number of auditory stimuli, the rate of auditory processing the person has to cope with and even other 'non-auditory' stimuli (lights, movements, etc.) that can contribute to sensory overload and result in auditory hypersensitivity. Training the ear to tolerate certain frequencies may bring some improvement in the short term but as it does not address the improvement of sensory processing of other channels that may be the main source of the person's overload, it is short-lived. AIT administered to the person whose main difficulties are rooted in auditory problems (i.e. they are the causes and not the symptoms) may produce 'miraculous' results, as it happened with Georgiana Stehli. When the primary problem is addressed and eliminated (or lessened), we can see immediate improvements in other systems as well, as they do not need to compensate for the impaired auditory channel and may get on with 'their own job'. On the other hand, if auditory problems result from the auditory system being compensation for other sensory systems with primary impairments, AIT does little to 'cure' the condition.

Irlen method

Helen Irlen has developed two methods to treat SS/IS: the use of coloured overlays to improve reading; and tinted glasses to improve visual perception of the environment.

Overlays are used to reduce perceptual distortions of printed text, such as, for instance, the dominance of the white background when the black print may fade into background. The optimal colour of the overlay is very individual and depends on each person's unique visual-perceptual sensitivities.

Irlen argues that visual-perceptual distortions can be minimized by the use of tinted non-optical lenses (Irlen filters) and has developed the Irlen Differential Perceptual Schedule to identify symptoms of SS/IS. It is believed that the lenses filter out those frequencies of the light spectrum to which a person may be uniquely sensitive (Irlen 1997). The use of colour, usually worn as tinted glasses (Irlen filters) appears to change the rate at which visual information is processed by the brain, thus reducing overload and hypersensitivity.

The Irlen Method consists of two steps:

Screening: Irlen has designed a special questionnaire, which serves as a screening instrument. The questionnaire has to be completed by either the individual themselves or a family member. Each questionnaire is evaluated to determine whether an individual is a candidate for the Irlen Method.

Testing: The correct colour is found. Usually it takes one to two sessions to determine the right colour. Irlen has designed a standardized set of procedures to determine the correct colour prescription for the overlay and the tinted lenses.

A large number of studies have reported positive results in using coloured filters (Robinson 1996). However, negative results have been reported (Winter 1987) and mixed outcomes (Cotton and Evans 1990) as well. At present there is no doubt that using coloured filters reduces print distortions experienced by many 'poor readers'. However, these filters do not solve the problem: improved print makes learning more effective but will not teach reading skills, and must be accompanied by appropriate reading correction methods.

Recently there have appeared reports about positive changes people with autism experience while using Irlen coloured lenses (see, for example,

Bogdashina 2001; Pemberton 1999; Waterhouse 2000) that give evidence that there are some visual-perceptual abnormalities in autism. The type of visual-perceptual deficits associated with autism is unique, and the distortions are varied, unpredictable and constantly changing.

Quite a few autistic individuals have reported positive changes in their visual hypersensitivity brought by the tinted filters (Blackman 2001; Sinclair 1998; Williams 1999). The positive changes are: perception with depth instead of a two-dimensional world; no fragmentation of visual information (coherence); meaning-blindness is rare; improvement in eye contact, reduced sensitivity to auditory stimuli; increased ability to understand language; the ability to use several channels at the same time (for example, to see *and* to hear). Vision becomes a reliable sense, the other senses do not need to compensate any more. As there is no need to compensate for visual overload, there is better processing of sound, touch or body connectedness. Autistic individuals who have benefited from the Irlen Method report seeing better, feeling more relaxed, less sensitive to bright lights; having fewer perceptual distortions; better small and gross motor coordination.

The Irlen Method is not a 'cure' for autism but rather one of the tools or compensatory strategies. It seems to work for those whose visual problems are overwhelming and helps slow down visual processing, thus helping to filter the information and in turn reducing the overload of other systems that compensate for unreliable vision.

At the age of eight, Alex, a boy with autism, was also diagnosed as suffering from SS/IS, and since the age of nine he has been wearing his Irlen lenses for six–eight hours a day. He was very hypersensitive to bright lights and could not tolerate fireworks, lightning and bright sunshine (Figure 7.1). After having worn his Irlen glasses for a few months his light sensitivity has considerably decreased and now he enjoys watching fireworks and theatrical performances, bright sunshine (Figure 7.2) but demands to wear his glasses while watching. However, it is still difficult for him to be in places where fluorescent lights are on. After 30–40 minutes he exhibits anxiety, aggression or sometimes sleepiness, even if he is wearing his glasses. When he is 'overloaded' his anger is directed at…the glasses. He hits them, complaining 'The glasses are not working.'

In the case of Alex, the decrease of visual distortions and light sensitivity led to the improvement of auditory sensitivities, the increase of an attention span, reading abilities and the improvement in motor coordination. It means that all senses are interconnected and one should work at the evaluation of the 'distortions' of the sensory system as a whole and find the ways to correct possible perceptual abnormalities of all the senses. Only if we know *what* needs correction can we find the ways to correct it.

Figure 7.1 Alex could not tolerate bright lights

Behavioural optometry

There have been suggested other methods to improve visual processing. One of these is behavioural optometry.

Behavioural optometry or vision therapy (sometimes it is also called 'occupational therapy for the eyes') is based on the principle that vision is a learned process and can be developed or enhanced at any age. Just as motor development, vision must follow certain steps of progression that may be

Figure 7.2 Alex is enjoying his day out in bright sunshine

hindered, distorted or even stopped due to injury, illness, sensory deprivation or other still unknown causes. If any disruption in visual development occurs it could be corrected by the use of special lenses, prisms, and vision therapy to enhance visual capabilities, reduce visual stress, prevent and rehabilitate vision problems. This approach is aimed at 'retraining' the eyes and the brain so they work together.

Vision dysfunction is often unrecognized and undiagnosed as the individuals may have 20/20 eyesight but distorted visual patterns. What makes the matter even more complicated is that many people have acquired compensatory strategies to cope with their visual difficulties. Specifically trained behavioural optometrists can identify visual dysfunctions, which are not identifiable by conventional eye tests. The symptoms of possible visual dysfunction include (from different sources):

- eyes that cross or turn
- tilting, turning the head
- closing or covering one eye in order to use only one eye
- peripheral vision
- blinking, grimacing, squinting the eyes
- finger flicking, spinning things and other visual stimulation behaviours
- short attention span, avoidance of close work
- headaches, dizziness, car sickness
- light sensitivity.

Vision therapy can be done at weekly sessions, with 'homework' assignments to train the skills learned during the sessions.

This approach has its sceptics who say that there is little proof that behavioural optometry can accomplish such a difficult task as organizing the brain by retraining eyes. However, anecdotal successful cases have been reported.

Holding therapy

In the late 1980s holding therapy was popularized and described as a 'miracle cure' for autism. These two magic words did inspire the parents to try it with their children. Though it brought extreme distress and suffering to both the child and the parents who had to observe the suffering of the child they were trying to help (cure?), the parents were told this was the price they had to pay for a 'miracle'. When the 'therapy' did not work, the therapist would simply tell the parents that they were not doing it often enough or that their hearts were not really in it when they did it (Siegel 1996).

When it works… Is it beneficial for the child? Let us listen to those for whom it 'worked'. Therese Joliffe wrote about her experience of 'successful holding therapy':

> To me the suffering was terrible and it achieved nothing... A claim by proponents of this therapy is that the children are much quieter and better behaved for a little while afterwards. My quietness was due to exhaustion and to my being disturbed so much as a result of the experience that I was shocked into a state of terrified quietness, where I could not think or do anything much for a while. (Joliffe, Lakesdown and Robinson 1992)

Isn't the price too high? The same (or even better) beneficial effect can be achieved by less stressful methods.

Claire Sainsbury (2000), a person with Asperger syndrome, believes that forced holding is not only not 'therapy', it is a form of abuse, a form of 'sensory rape'. Some professionals trying to justify holding therapy compare it with Temple Grandin's squeeze machine or describe it as a form of desensitization. It could not be further from the truth. The main differences are: the squeeze machine allows the user to control the touch and pressure and to be able to stop the stimulation when it becomes too overwhelming or intense. It is never forced.

Many autistic people are hypersensitive to tactile stimuli, especially light touch. Both hypersensitive and hyposensitive children benefit from deep pressure and often seek it themselves. They might crawl under tables, cushions, quilts and prefer tight clothes (Jackson 2002). Desensitization technique presupposes gradual exposure to touch and pressure in a way which is safe and enjoyable for a child. Forced holding has nothing to do with these techniques. It has nothing to do with bonding with mother, either.

'Hug machine'

Temple Grandin, who is very hypersensitive to touch, has discovered that deep pressure can help her reduce her hypersensitivity and the anxiety it causes. When a child, Temple would crave deep pressure, crawling under the sofa or wrapping herself in blankets. She could not get the 'right' amount of pressure from people because they were uncontrollable and either gave her too much or too little deep pressure.

The idea to create her 'hug/squeeze box' or 'hug/squeeze machine' came from her observation of cattle being branded in a squeeze chute at the farm of her relatives. Temple noticed that the cattle calmed down as soon as pressure was administered to them in the chute. She then designed and built her own device to administer pressure and control the amount and duration of it to achieve this calming effect. Gradually she was able to tolerate the machine holding her and her hypersensitivity to touch was slowly reduced.

The 'hug machine' is a device consisting of two padded side-boards, which are hinged near the bottom to form a V-shape. The person crawls inside and, by using a lever, provides the deep pressure stimulation. The lever operates an air cylinder, which pushes the sides together. The person can control the level of pressure he wants to stimulate.

Studies of the effectiveness of the 'hug machine' have produced some positive results. The researchers found a reduction of tension and anxiety resulted from the 'hug sessions'; the number of stereotypies decreased, more relaxed behaviour followed afterwards. The best candidates to use the machine are those with tactile hypersensitivity, hyposensitivity (seeking for deep pressure experiences) and those who cannot regulate their arousal state.

Some people need time to desensitize themselves while inside the machine (letting the sides touch them). When the nervous system becomes desensitized through gradual and slow stimulation, the experience of touch becomes pleasurable.

Sensory integration therapy

The goal of sensory integration therapy is described as facilitating the development of the nervous system's ability to process sensory input in a more normal way. The main principles of sensory integration therapy were introduced by Delacato (who called it treatment of sensory dysfunction) and Ayres. They were based on the assumption that many autistic children could be helped through gently applying sensory stimulation through five senses (Delacato 1974) or tactile, proprioceptive and vestibular stimulation (Ayres 1979). At present, some occupational therapists still rigorously follow Ayres's recommendations to work at the 'three major senses', while there are others who recognize the necessity to involve other senses as well.

SI approaches may be of various types:

1   Multi-sensory integration – the use of senses (vision, hearing, tactility, smell, taste, proprioception and vestibular system) in an integrated way, i.e. the use of several systems at once, for example, look and listen, rather than being single-channelled (mono-processing). However, it is important to remember that mono-processing is a strategy to avoid overload by using one channel at a time that is caused by the inability to filter out background and foreground information. In this case it is a symptom of the overload not the cause of it. That is why the original causes of sensory overload (which might be different for each individual) should be addressed.

2.   Desensitization, though not a cure, does provide more tolerance, increase speech and eye contact and decrease stereotypical, self-injurious and aggressive behaviours in some children. The sensory activities are aimed to raise the children's threshold for arousal. They are never forced but introduced gently in the form of games and pleasurable exercises. The therapist typically analyses the child's processing of vestibular, proprioceptive and tactile sensations in relation to the child's ability to learn and move and incorporates meaningful activities that provide specific sensory stimuli to elicit an adaptive response, thereby assisting the child in overall motor and conceptual learning (Fisher and Murray 1991). The change in environment is also recommended. To have an optimum effect, the sensory diet should be designed for the child's unique sensory processing needs (Wilbarger 1995).

Sensory diet is defined as a type of therapy that involves a planned and scheduled activity programme implemented by an occupational therapist. Each diet is designed to meet the needs of each particular child's nervous system. 'Just as the five main food groups provide daily nutritional requirements, a daily sensory diet fulfils physical and emotional needs' (Kranowitz 1998, p.187). A sensory diet stimulates the 'near' senses (tactile, vestibular and proprioceptive) with a combination of alerting, organizing and calming techniques.

For instance, hypersensitivity to touch is addressed through stroking a child with different textures (Ayres 1979). It should be done by an experienced therapist. A light touch increases arousal and overstimulation of the central nervous system. The pressure should be firm but gentle. Deep pressure stimulation is proved to be calming (Ayres 1979; King 1989). Different techniques are used to desensitize the child. For example, the Wilbarger Brushing Protocol, also known the Deep Pressure Proprioceptive Touch Technique, involves the use of a small brush and a massage protocol. With a special surgical brush the therapist makes firm, brisk movements over the body, especially the arms, hands, legs and feet. The brushing is followed by a technique of deep joint compression. As the child receives deep touch pressure the tactile receptors that are hypersensitive to light touch are depressed. Eventually, the child's tolerance to tactile stimulation increases.

Other techniques used in sensory integration therapy are tactile play (shaving cream and soap foam play, play dough); 'heavy work' activities (pushing and pulling a heavy box around the room; tug-of-war games; 'sandwiches' when a child is placed between two couch cushions and 'squished'); vestibular activities (large therapy balls for bouncing, rolling, jumping on).

An occupational therapist teaches the parents to use these techniques with a child at home for three to five minutes, six to eight times a day. As the child starts responding to touch more normally, the time of the sessions is reduced. The therapist should monitor the child's responsiveness to the strategies and, should any adverse reactions occur, the therapist should discontinue the activity and modify the treatment approach accordingly (Koomar and Bundy 1991).

Very often tactile stimulation may help different sensory systems work together and become more integrated. That can explain the necessity to feel the facilitator hand even on the shoulder to be able to communicate via facilitated communication. The supporters of SI therapy hypothesize that SI treatment can influence brain organization and brain change. As it is difficult to observe any changes in the brain, the only means to evaluate the effectiveness of the therapy is limited to observable behaviours. To complicate the matter, there is still no agreement about what to consider 'truly sensory integrative' treatments. As there are no clear definitions of SI and SID, the principles of the 'truly SI therapy' seem to change from author to author. For example, Cermak and Henderson (1999) exclude any studies which involve 'pure sensory stimulation' from the 'truly sensory integrative' treatments because they are inconsistent with the principles of SI the authors opted to choose as 'truly sensory integrative' ones, i.e. the characteristics of sensory integration procedures, proposed by Kimbal:

- active participation
- child directed
- individualized treatment
- purposeful activity
- need for adaptive response
- input varies based on child's response
- activity rich in proprioceptive, vestibular and tactile input
- implied or stated goal of improving processing and organization of sensation (not the teaching of specific skills)
- administered by a trained therapist (OT or PT). (Cermak and Henderson, 1999)

These characteristics restrict treatments to the 'main three senses' leaving vision and hearing out of the 'truly sensory integrative' interventions. It is necessary to mention, though, that many researchers and occupational therapists do include other senses in SI therapy.

In SI research, factors influencing the effectiveness of SI therapy have been identified:

- the child's age: children under six were reported to make rapid progress in therapy
- the diagnosis
- the severity of responsiveness to certain kinds of sensory input. (Ayres and Tickle 1980)

Aromatherapy

Aromatherapy is a therapeutic treatment using essential oils and massage. It stimulates the senses of smell, tactility and proprioception and can often bring relaxation. The repeated association of a particular smell with feeling calm and relaxed during a sensory-massage session can 'teach' relaxation (Longhorn 1993).

Autistic individuals who operate with 'smell pictures' and define objects, places and people by smell can be taught to react to particular smells (for example, to relax during sensory overload or anxiety).

This method is also used with music or 'cue' words – the same word or phrase repeated softly during relaxation sessions – and can be used at 'difficult times' when the person is distressed (Ellwood undated).

Sensory-massage can help to develop tolerance to touch and body awareness.

Chapter 8

Sensory Perceptual Profile

Differences in perception lead to a different perceptual world that inevitably is interpreted differently. We have to be aware of these differences and help autistic people to cope with painful sensitivities and develop their strengths ('perceptual superabilities') that are often unnoticed or ignored by non-autistic people.

Teachers and other professionals who work with autistic children need to recognize sensory differences in autism in order to select appropriate methods and plan intervention for these children.

As all the senses are integrated, deficiency in one may lead to disturbances in the other(s). It is, therefore, necessary to find out which senses and to which extent are deficient, and which senses can 'be relied on'.

In the 1960s–70s the batteries of 'perceptual tests' and screening tools were developed in order to identify 'perceptually handicapped' children. These tests were aimed at identifying lack of such skills as 'laterality', 'directionality', 'visual closure', 'ocular pursuit', 'temporal-spatial relations' but never addressed such perceptual phenomena as hyper- or hyposensitivity, inconsistency of perception, mono-processing, delayed perception, etc. The conventional auditory and visual acuity tests do not detect these problems.

There exist several standardized instruments for evaluating sensory integrative dysfunction, for example, the Sensory Integration and Praxis Tests for children between the ages of four years and eight years eleven months (Ayres 1989), the DeGangi-Berk Test of Sensory Integration for children aged three to five (Berk and DeGangi 1983), but these tests are sort of 'office tests'. They do not assess the child in natural settings and are aimed only at identifying deficits. Besides, the age limit does not allow assessment of the trends of sensory development and compensatory strategies acquired by the individual.

As it is difficult for autistic children to tolerate the test situation or understand what they are expected to do, these tests are not suitable for autistic children.

Recently quite a few informal assessments have been developed as screening tools for SI problems in the form of parent questionnaires that are aimed to reveal sensory-related problems.

The Sensory Profile Checklist-Revised (SPCR, Appendix 1) has been organized into a screening tool for compiling a Sensory Profile of an autistic child. Its descriptors are based on the information from personal accounts of autistic individuals and close observations of autistic children. The SPCR includes 20 categories through all 7 sensory systems to cover possible patterns of autistic people's sensory experiences. This 'inside-out' approach to the problem reveals that not all sensory experiences are dysfunctional, and some of them might be classified as 'superabilities' and considered as strengths rather than weaknesses. It has been found very useful to 'narrow' the terms to describe different sensory perceptions. For example, the statement 'the child is hypersensitive to visual stimuli' does not say much about this particular child's visual experiences, as the child's vision might be distorted, peripheral, too acute, etc. Distinguishing between different 'hypersensitivities' allows us to address that particular child's deficits while using his strengths.

Table 8.1 summarizes possible sensory experiences in autism singled out for the Sensory Profile.

Table 8.1 Possible Patterns Of Sensory Experiences In Autism

	Vision	*Hearing*	*Tactility*	*Smell*	*Taste*	*Proprioception*	*Vestibular*
1. Gestalt perception	Inability to filter visual stimuli	Inability to screen out background noise	Inability to distinguish between tactile stimuli of different intensity	Inability to distinguish between strong and weak smells	Inability to distinguish between strong and weak tastes	Inability to coordinate body position and movements of body parts	Inability to distinguish between 'inner' and 'outer' movements
2. Intensity with which the senses work	Hyper-, hypo-	Hyper-, hypo-	Hyper-, hypo-	Hyper-, hypo-	Hyper-, hypo-	Hyper-, hypo-	Hyper-, hypo-
3. Sensitivity to (disturbance by) some stimuli	Light/colour sensitivity Disturbance by some patterns	Disturbance by some sounds	Sensitivity to certain textures	Disturbance by some olfactory stimuli	Disturbance by some gustatory stimuli	Disturbance by some body positions	Intolerance of certain movements
4. Fascination with certain stimuli	Fascination with patterns, lights, colours	Fascination with sounds	Fascination with tactile stimuli	Fascination with smells	Fascination with flavours	Fascination with certain body movements	Excessive physical movements
5. Inconsistency of perception (fluctuation)	Fluctuation between hyper- and hypo-; 'in' –'out'	Fluctuation between hyper- and hypo-; 'in' –'out'	Fluctuation between hyper- and hypo-; 'in' –'out'	Fluctuation between hyper- and hypo-; 'in' –'out'	Fluctuation between hyper- and hypo-; 'in' –'out'	Fluctuation between hyper- and hypo-; 'in' –'out'	Fluctuation between hyper- and hypo-; 'in' –'out'

	Vision	Hearing	Touch	Smell	Taste	Body position	Movement
6. Fragmented perception (Partial perception)	Seeing 'in bits', prosopagnosia	Hearing 'in bits'	Feeling touch, cold/hot 'in bits'	Smelling 'in bits'	Tasting 'in bits'	Feeling only some parts of the body	'Uneven' movements
7. Distorted perception	Poor/distorted depth and space perception; seeing 2D world; distortions of shape, size	Hearing distorted sounds, etc.	Distorted tactile perception	Distorted olfactory perception	Distorted gustatory perception	Distorted perception of body	Distorted perception of body movements
8. 'Sensory agnosia' (difficulty interpreting a sense)	'Meaning-blindness'; feeling/acting 'blind'	'Meaning-deafness'; feeling/acting 'deaf'	'Touch deadness'	Difficulty interpreting smells	Difficulty interpreting tastes	Difficulty interpreting body position, body sensations, etc.	Difficulty interpreting body/head movements
9. Delayed perception	Delayed processing of visual stimuli	Delayed processing of auditory stimuli	Delayed processing of tactile stimuli	Delayed processing of smells	Delayed processing of tastes	Delayed processing of body postures, body sensations	Delayed processing of movement of head/body
10. Vulnerability to sensory overload	Visual overload	Sound overload	Tactile overload	Olfactory overload	Gustatory overload	Proprioceptive overload	Vestibular overload

	Visual	Auditory	Tactile	Olfactory	Gustatory	Proprioceptive	Vestibular
11. Mono-processing (number of channels working at a time)	Shutting down other senses while seeing	Shutting down other channels while hearing	Shutting down other channels while touching or being touched	Shutting down other senses while smelling	Shutting down other senses while tasting	Shutting down other senses while being aware of body position	Shutting down other channels while aware of body movements
12. Peripheral perception (avoidance of direct perception)	Peripheral vision, avoidance of eye contact	Hearing if listening to somebody indirectly	Peripheral tactile perception	Peripheral olfactory perception	Peripheral gustatory perception	Peripheral proprioceptive perception	Peripheral vestibular perception
13. Systems shutdowns	Visual 'whiteouts'	Auditory 'tuneouts'	Tactile 'tuneouts'	Olfactory 'tuneouts'	Gustatory 'tuneouts'	Proprioceptive 'tuneouts'	Vestibular 'tuneouts'
14. Compensating for unreliable sense by other senses	Checking visual perception by other senses	Checking auditory perception by other senses	Checking tactile perception by other senses	Checking olfactory perception by other senses	Checking gustatory perception by other senses	Checking proprioceptive perception by other senses	Checking vestibular perception by other senses
15. 'Losing oneself' in stimuli. Resonance	Merging, getting in resonance with lights, colours, patterns	Merging, getting in resonance with sounds	Merging, getting in resonance with tactile stimuli; feeling pain of other people	Merging, getting in resonance with smells	Merging, getting in resonance with tastes	Merging, getting in resonance with movements	In constant motion

	'Seeing' thoughts, emotions of other people; events that do not relate to oneself	'Hearing' thoughts of other people; events	'Feeling' events	'Olfactory hallucinations'	'Gustatory hallucinations'	Experiencing physical movements while being still	Experiencing movements of head/body while being still
16. Daydreaming	'Seeing' thoughts, emotions of other people; events that do not relate to oneself	'Hearing' thoughts of other people; events	'Feeling' events	'Olfactory hallucinations'	'Gustatory hallucinations'	Experiencing physical movements while being still	Experiencing movements of head/body while being still
17. Synaesthesia	Seeing sounds, smells, temperature, etc.	Hearing colours, flavours, touch, etc.	Seeing colours, hearing sounds while being touched	Smelling sounds, colours, etc.	Tasting shapes, colours, sounds, etc.	Involuntary body postures in response to visual, auditory, tactile, etc. stimuli	Involuntary body movements in response to visual, auditory, tactile, etc. stimuli
18. Perceptual memory	Visual ('photographic') memory	'Audiographic/sound' memory	Tactile memory	Olfactory memory	Gustatory memory	Proprioceptive memory	Vestibular memory
19. Associative ('serial') memory	Triggered by visual stimuli	Triggered by auditory stimuli	Triggered by tactile stimuli	Triggered by smells	Triggered by tastes	Triggered by body positions, movements	Triggered by motor activities
20. Perceptual thinking	Visual thinking ('thinking in pictures')	Thinking in 'auditory pictures'	Thinking in 'tactile images'	Thinking in 'olfactory images'	Thinking in 'gustatory images'	'Body positions, movements images'	Relating to head/body movements

The SPCR is completed by the parents of the child. However, while the input from the parents is very important, particularly regarding the child's sensory history and behaviour at home, it is also necessary to observe the child during sessions at school or at the clinic in order to consolidate the parental information and check some points marked in the SPCR as 'not sure'. The observation is conducted in the form of 'incident' sampling – each time the target behaviour occurs a box is ticked. To organize and summarize the observations Observation Checklists prove to be very useful. They include a list of behaviours (sensorisms) which should be checked for the child. At the stage of interpretations of the findings, the parents and the children should be actively involved. The discussions with the parents are vital as they help not only to compile the SPCR for their child but also to interpret the child's behaviours. The children should be encouraged to analyse their own behaviours and give their own interpretation of them through verbal explanation and/or drawings (how they feel and perceive the world).

The Sensory Perceptual Profile compiled for each child helps to:

- Identify the areas in which the child has (or had) problems but has learned to cope with them either by normalizing (desensitizing) the channel or by having acquired compensatory strategies. Using the data from 'Was True' column we can trace the history of the child's sensory development and identify the acquired strategies to cope with certain deficits.

- Identify domains of strength which will be used both to provide compensatory techniques for coping with painful and meaningless input paths and to provide 'communication channels' to bring the information to the child.

- Identify 'problem domains' in order to be desensitized or accommodated.

- Identify the preferred sensory modality that will be used as the 'gates' to bring information to the child. (For the majority of autistic children it is vision. However, some children exhibit preference for auditory, tactile or olfactory channels.)

- Select the appropriate intervention strategies in accordance with the child's strengths and weaknesses.

The data obtained from the SPCR can be presented in the form of specially worked out graphs – 'rainbows' – with the boxes, representing specific features experienced by the individuals, coloured in. The numbers in the graph coincide with the characteristics enumerated in the table. Different colours can be used for each sensory channel: for example, red for vision, orange for hearing, yellow for tactility, green for smell, blue for taste, indigo for proprioception, and violet for vestibular sense. The extent to which each channel is affected is demonstrated when the 'rainbows' are coloured in as the number of coloured sections correspond to the number of characteristics experienced by the individual. As all the senses are integrated, the deficiency in one may lead to disturbances in the other(s). 'Rainbows' are supposed to assist in finding out which sense(s) and to what extent are deficient and which ones are 'reliable' or 'superior'.

The reason the symbol of a rainbow was chosen to indicate probable sensory experiences was that many autistic people compare autism with a rainbow and describe the autistic world as a rainbow prism. Besides, it seems appropriate to show the Sensory Profile of an autistic individual in the form of curved lines rather than a straight line, as not all sensory differences are deficits; some are better described as superabilities (or gifts) that could be successfully used in the treatment of autistic people. Figures 8.1–8.4 show the 'rainbows' compiled for four children diagnosed as having autism. The graphs reveal the diversity of sensory problems experienced by each child, while the symptoms 'on the surface' (DSM-IV, ICD-10) are the same.

Treatment programmes that are appropriate and beneficial for one child may be painful and harmful for another. Thus, if the 'right' problem is addressed, the child gets more chances to benefit from the treatment.

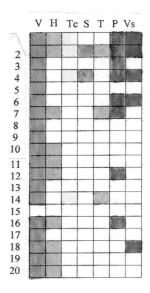
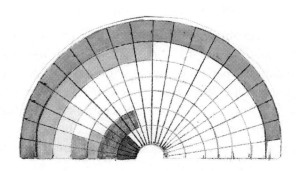

Figure 8.1 Alex's Rainbow

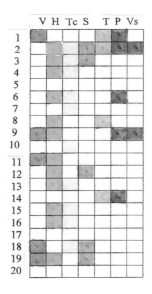
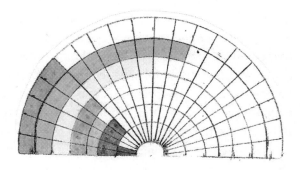

Figure 8.2 Vicky's Rainbow

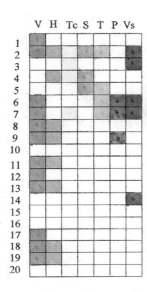

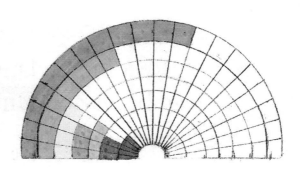

Figure 8.3 Helen's Rainbow

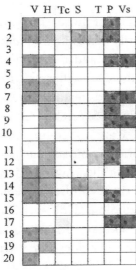

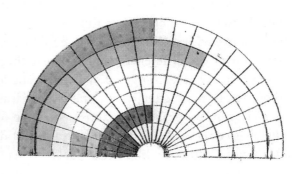

Figure 8.4 John's Rainbow

Chapter 9

Recommendations:
Rainbows and Umbrellas

> The role of professionals should be to help people use their natural processes to learn and grow. This might mean helping people develop strategies for dealing with sensory oversensitivities: using earplugs or colored lenses, adapting clothing to accommodate tactile sensitivities, providing opportunities for deep pressure or vestibular stimulation, etc. It might mean teaching self-monitoring and self-management of behavior and emotions. (Jim Sinclair 1998)

The ability to perceive stimuli in the environment accurately is basic to many areas of academic, communicative and social functioning. As autistic people do have 'differences' in this area, it is important for those who work and/or live with autistic children to be able to identify these and to understand how these differences might relate to the problems autistic individuals experience in learning and in general functioning. This will enable the provision of more effective programmes of learning and treatment.

The sensory problems in autism are often overlooked. As children are unable to cope with the demands of the world they are not equipped to deal with, they are likely to display behavioural problems, such as self-stimulation, self-injury, aggression, avoidance, rigidity, high anxiety, panic attacks, etc. It is important to remember that these children have no control over their problems, as they are caused by neurological differences.

The so-called low-functioning autistic individuals may have a near-normal brain trapped inside a sensory system that does not work properly and, as a result, not enough undistorted information gets through. It may be that the child's abnormal sensory functioning leads to secondary abnormalities in the brain development because of distorted sensory input or lack of sensory input (Grandin 1996a). The more the child shuts down the incoming stimuli, the more sensory deprivation he creates and the less opportunity he has to learn to interact with the world.

Because autism is a neurological disorder it causes some behaviours that a child cannot change without specific help. This is similar to hearing aids for deaf children, glasses for children with vision problems and wheelchairs for cerebral palsy children. Just as we never blame a blind child when he cannot name the colours of the pictures we show him, or expect a deaf child to come when we call him from two rooms away, we should not demand from a child whose disability is not straightforwardly visible to 'behave himself', but should try to find out the reason for his 'misbehaviour'. We accept that we cannot cure blindness and we do not waste time and effort teaching a visually impaired child to recognize colours using a bar of chocolate as a reward. We see our task to help a blind child function using different ways and compensatory strategies, and adjusting the environment to make it easier for him to orient in space. We accept and respect his disability, which, if appropriately addressed, does not interfere with the quality of life.

While people with 'visible' disabilities, such as, for example, visual /hearing impairments or cerebral palsy, are provided with special tools to lessen their problems (glasses, hearing aids, wheelchairs) autistic children with 'invisible' sensory processing problems are often denied any support to accommodate their difficulties. Whatever educational approach is implemented, sensory interventions are vital in order for the child to benefit from it. To effectively teach and treat autistic children it is necessary to understand how the qualitative differences of sensory perception associated with autism affect each particular child. Often it is not the treatment and the number of hours you work with your child, but in 'what perceptual world' you both are, i.e. whether you are in one and the same perceptual world or in two different ones.

First, we must understand how the child experiences the world through each of the channels and how he interprets what he sees, hears and feels, in order to design treatment programmes in accordance with his perceptual abilities and deficits. Understanding each particular person's specific difficulties and how they may affect this person's functioning is vital in order to adopt methods and strategies to help the person function in the community.

Analysing the information from the SPCR, along with observations and reports from people who know the child will provide an accurate picture of each particular child's strengths and weaknesses. It gives information about what the child currently can and cannot do, and allows setting priorities in his treatment programme.

There is a continuum of sensory processing problems in autism. Some people have severe sensory distortions while others may experience only mild but nevertheless confusing sensory problems. Nonverbal people usually have more severe sensitivities. The unique characteristics of each child will require unique individual strategies, techniques and environmental adjustments to be implemented. There is no single strategy for all autistic children as each of them exhibits a very individual sensory profile. Moreover, with age the strategy that was very useful for this particular child may not work any more and should be replaced by another to reflect the changes in the child's abilities to function.

There are two major sets of factors which may influence the child's level of functioning: negative factors and positive factors. Each set falls into two categories. The first category comprises personal (internal) characteristics of the child – both positive (the child's strengths and abilities) and negative (the child's weaknesses and deficits) characteristics. The second category is composed of environmental (external) factors: positive factors (resources and conditions helping the child to cope with his weaknesses and to develop his strength) and negative ones (interfering with the child's ability to cope). The aim of any intervention programme should be to create and/or develop both internal and external positive factors in order to counterbalance the negative ones.

The internal positive factors represent the child's strengths, preferences and interests. The internal negative factors include painful hypersensitivities and acquired strategies to cope with them that may lead to secondary impairments, for example, shutdowns. The balance between positive and negative characteristics may change with age and development though some general features are typically found in all people with autism (such as perceptual thinking/perceptual memory). While developing programmes it is necessary to keep in mind the child's strengths. Building on the child's natural resources and the strategies he has acquired will increase the child's competence and level of functioning. The preferences and interests will serve as motivators, reinforcers and 'first aid' in the case of sensory overload. Often the behaviours that seem challenging may hide the child's strengths and may be 'shaped' into assets rather than problems.

Using the SPCR we may identify the negative factors within and outside the child in order to eliminate them and we may explore the ways to use positive factors available in order to help the child to learn and function in the community. This information will also help parents and professionals who work with the child learn how to relate to the child in order to avoid undesirable 'by-products' of sensory processing difficulties – tantrums, aggression, etc.

We can get a lot of information from watching repetitive behaviours. These behaviours are the key to understanding the way the child experiences the world, the problems he faces and the strategies he has acquired to cope with his difficulties. Consciously or unconsciously the child tries to regulate the environment and his responses to it and acquires defensive strategies and compensations for his deficits. The child shows us his way to cope with his problems.

However, one of the difficulties in interpreting the child's behaviour caused by sensory processing differences is our own 'non-autistic' sensory function. We have to train ourselves to perceive and understand the world from the individual's perspective. Only then will we join the person 'on his territory', in his perceptual world, and will not have to function in two parallel ones.

Repetitive behaviours in autism are multi-functional. They may be:

- defensive: in order to reduce the pain caused by hypersensitivities

- self-stimulatory: to improve the input in the case of hyposensitivity

- compensatory: to interpret the environment in the case of 'unreliable' channels

- just pleasurable experiences that help to withdraw from a confusing environment.

These behaviours will change with the child's changing abilities. As deficits in one area interact and affect other areas, improving functioning in one sensory modality may bring improvements in the others. For instance, reducing visual hypersensitivities (with the help of tinted glasses, for example) may make auditory and tactile stimuli less overwhelming.

By looking at how the child reacts, it is possible to reconstruct and assess the child's problems in various sensory channels. The child's 'self-prescribed' movements (rocking, flapping hands, jumping) give a very clear idea of what the child needs.

For example, if a child frequently covers his ears (even if you do not hear any disturbing sounds) it means his hearing is hypersensitive, and it is your job to find out which sounds/noises disturb him. If a child flicks his fingers in front of his eyes, he might have problems with hypersensitive or hyposensitive vision. Children who like crowds and noisy places either have mild sensory problems or are hyposensitive. Autistic children are often engaged in stereotyped activities. If these activities serve as a protective mechanism to shut down the sensory stimuli because they are painful or overwhelming, the job of an educator (or a parent) is to decrease sensory bombardment.

Let us look at some possible interpretations of the SPCR.

'Gestalt'

Difficulty in filtering background and foreground information caused by gestalt perception leads to rigidity of thinking and lack of generalization. Autistic people can perform in exactly the same situation with exactly the same prompts but fail to apply the skill if anything in the environment, routine or prompt has been even slightly changed. For instance, the child can perform the task if he is being touched on the shoulder and fails if he has not been given the prompt. Alternatively, a familiar room may seem different and threatening if the furniture has been slightly rearranged. These children need sameness and predictability to feel safe in their environment. If something is not the same, it changes the whole gestalt of the situation and they do not know what they are expected to do. It brings confusion and frustration. The strategy is to always communicate to the child beforehand, in a way he can understand (i.e. visual, tactile, etc.) what and why will be changed. Changes should be gradual, with the child's active participation.

On the perceptual level the inability to filter foreground and background information may bring sensory overload. Children are bombarded with sensory stimuli. They are 'drowned' in them. For individuals with 'auditory gestalt' perception, for example, a lot of effort has to be made to understand what is being said if there is more than one conversation going on in the room or more than one person speaking at a time. They are bombarded with noises from all directions. If they try to screen out the background noise they also screen out the voice of the person they try to listen to. The task should be to find out which modality does not filter the information and make the environment 'visually/auditorily, etc. simple'. The next step would be to teach the person 'to break the picture (visual/auditory/tactile/olfactory/ gustatory)' into meaningful units.

Hyper-/hyposensitivities

Each of the senses (vision, hearing, tactility, smell, taste, proprioception, vestibular system) should be assessed to determine if the child is hyper- or hyposensitive. Depending on the sensitivity, the objectives should be both to desensitize the child's ability to tolerate the stimuli (internal factors) and to provide the aids to help him cope with 'offensive' stimuli (tinted glasses, earplugs, etc.). Desensitization is aimed to increase sensory tolerance very gradually through pleasurable activities.

There are many challenging behaviours (self-injury, tantrums, aggression) that can be dealt with effectively by simply changing the environment. Consider the level of 'sensory pollution'. In the case of hypersensitivities, even a 'visually/auditorily' quiet environment may cause overstimulation and challenges for the child. Autistic people must be protected from painful stimuli. For example, fluorescent lights might be replaced by ordinary bulbs (in the case of visual hypersensitivity); school bells might be disconnected until the child's auditory hypersensitivity is reduced, etc. If the child is hypersensitive, it is important to keep visual and auditory distraction to a minimum. We should always remember that if we cannot hear/see/smell/feel some stimuli, it does not mean that the child 'is being stupid' if distressed by 'nothing at sight'.

Tactile hypersensitivities should be addressed by choosing clothes and fabrics the child can tolerate. Wearing tight clothes that apply pressure helps to reduce self-stimulatory behaviours. As hypertactile children are frightened by light touch, especially if it is unpredictable, always approach the child from the front to prepare him visually for possible touch.

Always monitor a number of simultaneous stimuli. If there are several conversations in the same room, plus fans working, plus people moving around, plus a fan working two rooms away…the child with sensory hypersensitivities is sure to be overwhelmed.

If a child is hyposensitive, provide extra stimulation through the channels that do not get enough information from the environment. Encourage physical exercises (swinging, climbing), pushing/carrying heavy objects.

As each child is unique, we very often find children with hyper- or hyposensitivities in one and the same classroom. The knowledge of each child's sensitivities can help the teacher to plan the activities and address each child's particular needs. It is often very difficult to adjust the environment to satisfy the needs of several children as the same stimuli may cause pain in some children and bring pleasurable experiences in others.

Sensitivity to (disturbance by) some stimuli

Identify which sensory stimuli may interfere with the child's capability to cope and either reduce or eliminate them or, if impossible, provide 'sensory aids' (tinted glasses, earplugs) or protect the child with a 'sensory umbrella' – modifications and adaptations of the environment to meet the child's needs. Remember, what we think is enjoyable (for example, fireworks) may be fearful or overwhelming to an autistic child.

Reported strategies to cope with light sensitivity are turning off any unnecessary lighting (especially fluorescent lighting), using lamps rather than overhead lights, low wattage light bulbs and tinted lenses.

Be aware of the colours and patterns of the clothes you are wearing and of your perfume.

The fear of a stimulus that 'hurts' is often the cause of many challenging behaviours. The antecedents cannot be easily identified. Sometimes we cannot see/hear/feel them as our senses are too 'normal'. Sometimes these are 'possible future antecedents'. Some autistic children try to break things (telephone or alarm clock, for example) that can produce painful stimuli. They do it as a protective reaction. The staff working with the child must consider not only immediate environmental threats for the child but also any potential factors that can cause painful experiences. It is useful to make a list of possible threatening/painful stimuli for each child, no matter how common and unthreatening they might seem to us: school bells, fire alarms, fans, dogs barking, babies crying, etc. Always warn a child about the possibility of the stimulus he is fearful of and show the source of it.

Joe, an 11-year-old autistic boy, could not tolerate the high-pitched voice of one of his classmates. As soon as Mike appeared in the doorway, Joe would rush outside covering his ears and screaming. If the door was locked he got under the table with his hands over his head. Mike, a teenager with AS, was very upset: 'I didn't even say anything. Why is he afraid of me?' Very gradually Joe was 'desensitized' to Mike's voice: Joe was encouraged to watch Mike's lips. Though he still found it difficult to tolerate the voice, the predictability and watching the source of it made it easier for Joe to cope with it.

Fascination with certain stimuli

Make a list of pleasant stimuli, to be used in the 'case of emergency' – to calm down the child after a painful/stressful experience. If you think the activities (behaviours) or materials the child uses for 'self-treatment' are inappropriate, identify their function and replace them with more appropriate ones. Remember that the stimulus that is pleasurable for one child may be a cause of distress for the other.

Inconsistency of perception (fluctuation)

The impact of environmental factors (both positive and negative) will vary with the age and circumstances of each child. At times it may appear that everything goes well, at other times the child may exhibit challenging behaviours under similar environmental conditions.

Fragmented perception

Routine and rituals help to facilitate understanding of what is going on and what is going to happen. Introduce any change very slowly and always explain beforehand what and why is happening differently. Structure and routines make the environment predictable and easier to control.

If a person is prosopagnostic, introduce yourself each time you see him. Wearing the same clothes and hairstyle facilitates 'recognition'.

Sensory agnosia (difficulty interpreting a sense)

Though they can see adequately, some autistic people may often have limited comprehension of what is seen when they are focused on something else. For example, they may be able to recognize the location of pieces of furniture in space to avoid bumping into them, but may not be able to identify what these objects are unless some cues (verbal or otherwise) are provided. Sometimes they cannot even identify people as people and may be startled by unexpected movements of 'noisy objects'. In the state of sensory agnosia they need similar aids as visually/auditory impaired people.

Delayed processing

Give people time to take in your question/instruction and work out their response. Do not interrupt. Be aware that autistic people require more time than others to shift their attention between stimuli of different modalities and they find it extremely difficult to follow rapidly changing social interactions.

Vulnerability to sensory overload

A child vulnerable to sensory overload needs to be in control of his environment. Learning to recognize early signs of coming sensory overload is very important. It is better to prevent it than to 'deal with the consequences'. A child may need a quiet place (the 'isle of safety') to recover, where he can go to 'recharge his batteries' from time to time.

Teach the child how to recognize the internal signs of the overload, how to control the state of his 'inner cup' and how to use strategies (for example, relaxation) to prevent the problem. A 'First Aid Kit' (for sensory overload) should always be at hand. Possible contents might be sunglasses, earplugs, squeezy toys, favourite toys, 'I need help' card.

Mono-processing (number of senses working at a time)

A child with mono-processing may have problems with multiple stimuli. Find out which channel 'is open' at the moment. Always present information in the child's preferred modality. If you are not sure what it is or which channel 'is on' at the moment (in the case of fluctuation), use multi-sensory presentation and watch which modality 'works'. Remember that they could switch channels.

Peripheral perception (avoidance of central/direct perception)

Never force eye contact. Use an indirectly confrontational approach, especially involving hypersensitive modalities. Indirectly confrontational communication can mean that if something needs explaining or showing, the person explaining or showing can do so as if out loud to themselves, addressing the wall or the floor, or his shoes, or the objects relating to the demonstration. The person with a problem of overload should be allowed, similarly, to address and interact with you through speaking out loud with you 'in mind'. Gradually, bridges can be built from indirectly to more directly confrontational interaction and communication (Williams 1996).

When hypersensitivity of the affected sensory channel is addressed and lessened, direct perception becomes easier. For example, an autistic boy whose visual hypersensitivity was intolerable and often painful was prescribed Irlen tinted glasses. After having worn them for a few months his eye contact improved from none to several seconds, and his 'visual behaviour' (using his eyes to look instead of using other senses to compensate for painful, and therefore often useless visual perception) became apparently better.

Systems shutdowns

If the sensory stimulation is overwhelming autistic people can shut their systems off. To avoid painful sounds they shut down hearing. (Though certain frequencies cannot be shut down.) Continuous noises (fans, microwave, heating) that do not bother other people may be very annoying. To shut down the painful channel they may engage in stereotypic behaviours, or deliberately distract themselves through other channels (for example, touching objects when hearing is overwhelming) or withdraw altogether.

Compensating for unreliable sense by other senses

Let the child use the sensory modality he prefers (for example, smell, touch) to 'check' his perception. With appropriate treatment and environmental adjustments to decrease hypersensitivities they gradually learn to use their sense organs properly – eyes to see, ears to listen, etc.

'Resonance', synaesthesia

In many ways 'autistic perception' is superior to that of non-autistics. Autistic individuals with their heightened senses can often appreciate colour, sound, texture, smell, taste to a higher degree than people around them. Their gifts and talents should be nurtured and not ridiculed, as is often the case. Let them use their ways to explore the world.

Perceptual memory. Perceptual thinking

Choose methods of instruction to match the child's learning style, for example, visual aids for 'visual thinkers', audiotapes for 'auditory thinkers', learning through movements, etc. The preferred channel will be our 'gate' to reach the child. Autistic children learn better with concrete information, whether it is visual, auditory, tactile, etc.

Conclusion

As some sensory dysfunction is present in all individuals with autism it would benefit parents of autistic children and professionals working with them to become more knowledgeable about the sensory perceptual problems they experience and possible ways to help them.

However, we need to stop trying to change them into 'normals' and to adapt to our world. The aim of any intervention should be to help autistic individuals to cope with their problems and to learn to function in the community. Whatever treatment programme or therapy is used, it does not make them less autistic. However, increased self-knowledge can lead to better compensations for one's difficulties, which in turn may decrease symptoms and make the autism less disabling (Gerland 1998). There is usually some natural progress in autistic children as they grow (Kanner 1971). Some of Kanner's patients became very high-functioning as adults even though they were not given any special treatment. These people found ways to cope with their problems and could function quite successfully.

The type of intervention should depend on the type and severity of sensory problems the child experiences. The intensity of treatment should be in direct proportion with the child's ability to cope with sensory stimulation.

As the Sensory Profile of each individual is unique, what works for one child may be not only painful but also harmful for another. That is why some methods (like, for example, Lovaas's Applied Behaviour Analysis Programme) work for some children and bring no improvement in others.

Parents often confess that what was intolerable about their child's behaviour was that it seemed meaningless. When they could understand the reason for this behaviour it did not seem strange or disturbing any more. This brings acceptance and respect for the autistic person's efforts to 'make sense' of the world.

Whatever approach/treatment is chosen, the person working with the child should make the environment sensorily safe for the child and try to 'move in the same sensory world'. Many behaviours that interfere with learning and social interaction are in fact protective or sensory defensive responses of the child to 'sensory pollution' in the environment.

Autistic people are vulnerable to being abused. They have to live in a world which is not designed for them, and they have to deal with people who, while being aware of the difficulties they experience, often overlook the effort they are making trying to survive in the world which is not designed for them. If we look at their 'bizarre' behaviours and responses through their eyes, they make sense. Our behaviours may equally seem 'bizarre' to autistic persons. For example, how could one enjoy fireworks if your eyes are hit with 'bunches of bright arrows' and the sound in your ears 'tears them raw'? We often do not understand the 'autistic perspective', the problems they experience. And sometimes our 'treatment' does more harm than good. Let us take some examples.

A family were struggling to find the solution to a challenging behaviour of an eight-year-old autistic boy. The boy removed his clothes at any opportunity no matter where he was. The mother asked for advice from a 'specialist'. And the advice was to encourage (?) the boy to keep his clothes on and reward him (with a chocolate biscuit) when he complies. If we look at this situation from the 'autistic perspective', tactile processing problems are obvious. The boy himself was aware of which fabric would 'hurt' him and tried to protect himself. His 'clues' were not recognized by the people involved. We could interpret the intervention as follows: a person with broken legs is encouraged to run and promised a reward of a chocolate biscuit. Would you run?

Another situation: at one of the autistic provisions, a teaching support assistant is happily whistling and singing. Joe, an 11-year-old autistic boy, is rocking back and forth. He covers his ears with his hands, but it does not seem to work and he pushes his index fingers inside his ears. No effect.

Then he pleads with his 'helper': 'Laura, stop singing, please. Stop it!' The reaction of the support worker? 'Why should I? Don't be stupid, Joe.' If we look at the same situation from Joe's perspective, we could interpret it as a sensory assault of the child. For this boy the 'singing' (whether it was the pitch of the voice or the sounds of whistling he could not tolerate) physically hurt his ears, as if the helper threw stones or litter at him. So why should she stop?

The sensory environment is very important for autistic people. They lack the ability to adjust to sensory assaults other people accept as normal. If we accommodate it and try to 'keep it clean' in order to meet their very special needs, the world could become more comfortable for them. With sensory needs met, problem behaviour becomes less of an issue. If there were no risk of being attacked, you would not need defence. To make the world safer for autistic individuals the price would not be too high – 'just stop singing' when they ask you to. And if they cannot ask because of their communication problems, use your knowledge and imagination to find out what they need.

Some questions remain: How many of the behavioural characteristics listed as diagnostic criteria for autism are symptoms of sensory dysfunction? How could children develop if these problems are addressed as early as they are labelled autistic? How could we enter their perceptual world and bring them into ours?

This book shows a possible direction to follow in the field of sensory perceptual dysfunction in autism. Besides, it could be a starting point for selection of methods and, probably, working out new ones, in order to address the individual needs of each particular child. And last, but not least, I hope this reconstruction of the sensory world of autism will give the readers some idea of the way autistic people perceive the world and will make non-autistics understand that the way they see the environment is not necessarily the only way to see it.

Sensory Profile Checklist Revised (SPCR)

Name of child_____Birthdate _____

Diagnosed _____When? _____ Where? _____

PURPOSE: This checklist is designed for completion by parents of children who have been diagnosed as having Autism Spectrum Disorder (ASD). The SPCR is intended to clarify the sensory experiences of such children and to draw a sensory profile ('Rainbow') in order to identify possible sensory strengths and weaknesses that would be helpful in selecting appropriate methods of teaching and treatment.

INSTRUCTIONS: Please tick the appropriate answer to indicate the statement described as:

- **WT** – was true in any time in the past: in brackets, specify the age of the child when the statement was true, e.g. (two–five yrs)

- **T** – true now (if it was true and is true now, tick both answers)

- **F** – false (if the statement is not true)

- **NS** – not sure or do not know.

Additional information is welcome: write it near the question, or copy the question number on a blank sheet of paper and add the information there.

Please try to answer all questions.

No	Behaviours	WT	T	F	NS
1	Resists any change				
2	Notices every tiny change in the environment				
3	Does not recognize a familiar environment if approaches it from a different direction				
4	Does not recognize people in unfamiliar clothes				
5	Is not fooled by optical illusions				
6	Constantly looks at minute particles, picks up smallest pieces of fluff				
7	Dislikes dark and bright lights				
8	Is frightened by sharp flashes of light, lightning, etc.				
9	Looks down most of the time				
10	Covers, closes, or squints eyes at bright light				
11	Is attracted to lights				
12	Looks intensely at objects and people				
13	Moves fingers or objects in front of eyes				
14	Is fascinated with reflections, bright coloured objects				
15	Runs a hand around the edge of the object				
16	Perimeter hugging				
17	Gets easily frustrated/tired under fluorescent lights				
18	Gets frustrated with certain colours (Specify:)				
19	Is fascinated with coloured and shining objects (Specify:)				
20	May respond differently (pleasure – indifference – distress) to the same visual stimuli (lights, colours, visual patterns, etc.)				
21	Selects for attention minor aspects of objects in the environment instead of the whole thing (e.g. a wheel rather than a whole toy car, etc.)				
22	Gets lost easily				
23	Fears heights, stairs, escalators				

24	Has difficulty catching balls				
25	Appears startled when being approached suddenly				
26	Makes compulsive repetitive hand, head, or body movements that fluctuate between near and far				
27	Hits/rubs eyes when distressed				
28	Feels/acts blind				
29	Ritualistic behaviour				
30	Response to visual stimuli is delayed (e.g. fails to close eyes when the light is being switched on, etc.)				
31	Any experiences are perceived as new and unfamiliar, regardless of the number of times the child has experienced the same thing				
32	Sudden outbursts of self-abuse/tantrums or withdrawal in response to visual stimuli				
33	Does not seem to see if listening to something				
34	Avoids direct eye contact				
35	Appears to be a mindless follower				
36	Surprises with knowing 'unknown' information				
37	Smells, licks, touches, or taps objects				
38	Seems to be absorbed (merged) with lights, colours, patterns				
39	Seems to know what other people (who are not present) are doing				
40	Covers/rubs/blinks, etc. eyes in response to a sound/touch/smell/taste/movement				
41	Complains about (is frustrated with) the 'wrong' colours of letters/numbers, etc. on coloured blocks, etc.				
42	Displays a good visual memory				
43	Reactions are triggered by lights, colours, patterns				
44	Easily solves jigsaw puzzles				
45	Remembers routes and places				

46	Memorizes enormous amounts of information at a glance				
47	Poor at mathematics				
48	Learns nouns first				
49	Has difficulties with adverbs and prepositions				
50	Idiosyncratic patterns in language development (e.g. names one thing to denote the other, etc.)				
51	Gets easily frustrated when trying to do something in a noisy, crowded room				
52	Does not seem to understand instructions if more than one person is talking				
53	Covers ears at many sounds				
54	Is a very light sleeper				
55	Is frightened by animals				
56	Dislikes thunderstorm, sea, crowds				
57	Dislikes haircut				
58	Avoids sounds and noises				
59	Makes repetitive noises to block out other sounds				
60	Bangs objects, doors				
61	Likes vibration				
62	Likes kitchen and bathroom				
63	Likes traffic, crowds				
64	Is attracted by sounds, noises				
65	Tears paper, crumples paper in the hand				
66	Makes loud rhythmic noises				
67	Gets frustrated with certain sounds (Specify:)				
68	Tries to destroy/break objects producing sounds (clock, telephone, musical toy, etc.)				
69	Is fascinated with certain sounds (Specify:)				
70	May respond differently (pleasure – indifference – distress) to the same auditory stimuli (sounds, noises)				

71	Hears a few words instead of the whole sentence				
72	Pronunciation problems				
73	Unable to distinguish between some sounds				
74	Hits ears when distressed				
75	Feels/acts deaf				
76	Response to sounds, questions, instructions is delayed				
77	Echolalia in monotonous, high-pitched, parrot-like voice				
78	Sudden outbursts of self-abuse/tantrums or withdrawal in response to auditory stimuli				
79	Does not seem to hear if looking at something				
80	Reacts to instructions better when they are 'addressed to the wall'				
81	Looks for the source of the sound				
82	Seems to be absorbed (merged) with sounds				
83	Seems to be able to 'read' thoughts, feelings, etc. of others				
84	Complains about 'non-existent' conversations, sounds				
85	Covers/hits ears in response to lights, colours/touch, texture/smell/taste/movement				
86	Complains about (is frustrated with) a sound in response to colours/textures/touch/scent/flavour/movement				
87	Displays a good auditory memory (for nursery rhymes, songs, etc.)				
88	Reactions are triggered by sounds/words				
89	Uses idiosyncratic routinized responses				
90	Uses songs, commercials, etc. to respond				
91	Cannot keep track of conversation				
92	Composes musical pieces, songs				
93	Unable to distinguish between tactile stimuli of different intensity (e.g. light and rough touch)				

94	Resists being touched				
95	Cannot tolerate new clothes; avoids wearing shoes				
96	Overreacts to heat/cold/pain				
97	Avoids getting messy				
98	Dislikes food of certain texture (Specify:)				
99	Moves away from people				
100	Insists on wearing the same clothes				
101	Likes pressure, tight clothing				
102	Seeks pressure by crawling under heavy objects, etc.				
103	Hugs tightly				
104	Enjoys rough and tumble play				
105	Prone to self-injuries				
106	Low reaction to pain, temperature				
107	Cannot tolerate certain textures (Specify:)				
108	Is fascinated with certain textures (Specify:)				
109	May respond differently (pleasure – indifference – distress) to the same tactile stimuli (clothes, touch, heat, pain, etc.)				
110	Complains about parts of the clothes				
111	Hits/bites themselves when distressed				
112	Feels/acts numb				
113	Sudden outbursts of self-abuse/tantrums or withdrawal in response to tactile stimuli				
114	Does not seem to feel being touched if looking at/listening to something				
115	Fails to define either texture or location of touch				
116	Can tolerate only 'instrumental' (not 'social') touch				
117	Sometimes does not react to any tactile stimuli				
118	Seems to be absorbed (merged) with certain textures				
119	Seems to feel pain of others				

120	Complains about being touched/hot/cold, etc. in the absence of the stimuli				
121	Complains about (is frustrated with) feeling colours, sound, etc. when being touched				
122	Complains about (is frustrated with) feeling being touched when being looked at				
123	Complains about (is frustrated with) backache, etc./heat/cold in colourful/noisy/crowded places				
124	Displays a good tactile memory				
125	Reactions are triggered by textures/touch/temperature				
126	Unable to distinguish between strong and weak odours				
127	Toileting problems				
128	Runs from smells				
129	Smells self, people, objects, etc.				
130	Smears/plays with faeces				
131	Seeks strong odours				
132	Bedwetting				
133	Cannot tolerate certain smells (Specify:)				
134	Is fascinated with some smells (Specify:)				
135	May respond differently (pleasure – indifference – distress) to the same smells				
136	Complains about smells of some pieces of food while ignoring the rest				
137	Hits nose when distressed				
138	Has difficulty in interpreting smells				
139	Response to smells is delayed				
140	Sudden outbursts of self-abuse/tantrums or withdrawal in response to smells				
141	Does not seem to feel smell when looking/listening, etc.				

142	Avoids direct smells				
143	Sometimes does not react to any smell				
144	Inspects food before eating				
145	Seems to be absorbed (merged) with smells				
146	Complains/talks about 'non-existent' smells				
147	Covers/rubs/hits nose in response to a visual/auditory stimulus/touch/taste/movement				
148	Complains about (is frustrated with) the smell in response to a visual/auditory stimulus/touch/taste/movement				
149	Displays a good memory for smells				
150	Reactions are triggered by smells				
151	Unable to distinguish between strong and weak tastes				
152	Poor eater				
153	Uses the tip of the tongue for tasting				
154	Gags/vomits easily				
155	Craves certain (plain) foods				
156	Eats anything (pica)				
157	Mouths and licks objects				
158	Eats mixed food (e.g. sweet and sour)				
159	Regurgitates				
160	Cannot tolerate certain food (Specify:)				
161	Is fascinated with certain tastes (Specify:)				
162	May respond differently (pleasure – indifference – distress) to the same food				
163	Is confused with (complains about) the food he used to like				
164	Has difficulty in interpreting tastes				
165	Response to tastes is delayed				
166	Sudden outbursts of self-abuse/tantrums or withdrawal in response to taste				

167	Does not feel any taste while eating something and looking at/listening to something				
168	A very careful eater				
169	Sometimes does not react to any taste				
170	Seems to be absorbed (merged) with certain food				
171	Complains/talks about 'non-existent' taste in mouth				
172	Makes swallowing movements in response to a visual/auditory stimulus/touch/smell/movement				
173	Complains about (is frustrated with) some tastes in response to a visual/auditory stimulus/touch/smell/movement				
174	Displays a good memory for tastes				
175	Reactions are triggered by certain food				
176	Clumsy; moves stiffly				
177	Odd body posturing (places the body in strange positions)				
178	Difficulty manipulating small objects (e.g. buttons)				
179	Turns the whole body to look at something				
180	Low muscle tone				
181	Has a weak grasp; drops things				
182	A lack of awareness of body position in space				
183	Unaware of their own body sensations (e.g. does not feel hunger)				
184	Bumps into objects, people				
185	Appears floppy; often leans against people, furniture, walls				
186	Stumbles frequently; has tendency to fall				
187	Rocks back and forth				
188	Cannot tolerate certain movements/body positions				
189	Is often engaged in complex body movements, esp. when frustrated or bored				
190	May have different muscle tone (low – high)				

191	Pencil lines, letters, words, etc. are uneven (e.g. sometimes too tight, sometimes too faint)				
192	Complains about limbs, parts of the body				
193	Difficulty with hopping, jumping, skipping, riding a tricycle/bicycle				
194	Does not seem to know what their body is doing				
195	Very poor at sports				
196	Tires very easily, esp. when in noisy/bright places, or when standing				
197	Does not seem to know the position of the body in space/what the body is doing, when looking at/listening to/talking				
198	Has difficulty imitating/copying movements				
199	Does not seem to know how to move their body (unable to change body position to accommodate task)				
200	Watches their feet while walking				
201	Watches their hands while doing something				
202	Seems to be absorbed with body movements				
203	Complains about 'non-existent' physical experiences (e.g. 'I am flying', etc.)				
204	Involuntary postures of the body in response to a visual/auditory stimulus/smell/taste/touch				
205	Displays a very good proprioceptive memory (e.g. understands directions better if produces exact movements they have to do in order to follow these directions)				
206	Reactions are triggered by body positions/movements				
207	Mimics the actions when instructions are being given				
208	Resists change to head position/movement				
209	Fearful reactions to ordinary movement activities (e.g. swings, slides, merry-go-round, etc.)				
210	Has difficulty with walking or crawling on uneven or unstable surfaces				

211	Dislikes head upside down				
212	Becomes anxious or distressed when feet leave the ground				
213	Enjoys swings, merry-go-round				
214	Spins, runs round and round				
215	Fears falling or height				
216	Spins, jumps, rocks, etc. esp. when frustrated or bored				
217	May respond differently (pleasure – indifference – distress) to the same movement activities (swings, slides, spinning, etc.)				
218	Resists new motor activities				
219	Tiptoeing				
220	Becomes disoriented after a change in head position				
221	Seems oblivious to risks of heights, etc.				
222	Holds head upright, even when leaning or bending over				
223	Gets nauseated or vomits from excessive movement (swings, merry-go-round, cars, etc.)				
224	Does not seem to mind any movements when looking at/listening to something/talking				
225	Avoids balancing activities				
226	Becomes disoriented in noisy/bright places, or after physical activities				
227	Rocks unconsciously during other activities (e.g. watching a video)				
228	Inspects the surface before walking on it				
229	Appears to be in constant motion				
230	Involuntary movements of the body in response to a visual/auditory stimulus/smell/taste/touch				
231	Experiences movement while being still (e.g. 'I am flying' while being in bed)				
232	Reactions are triggered by motor activities				

Key for Decoding the Checklist

This key will aid you in completing the chart and rainbow.

If you have ticked the 'True' box for a question in the Sensory Profile Checklist then you will need to colour in the corresponding box in the chart. For example, if you have answered question 15 as 'True' then you colour in box 2 in the V column. Some questions in the profile relate to the same box in the chart. For example, if you have answered 'True' to either question 76 or 77, colour in the box 9 in the H column.

Once you have completed the chart, count the number of coloured boxes in the corresponding section. Colour in the same number of boxes in the corresponding section of the rainbow. For example, if you have coloured in ten boxes in the V column, then colour in ten boxes of the V section of the rainbow.

V – Vision   T – Taste
H – Hearing   P – Proprioception
Tc – Tactility   Vs – Vestibular
S – Smell

1	V1; V6
2	V1
3	V1; V6
4	V1; V6
5	V1
6–9 (hyper-)	V2
10	V2; V3
11–16 (hypo-)	V2
17–18	V3
19	V4
20	V5
21–22	V6
23	V7; Vs7
24	V7; P7
25–27	V7
28	V8
29	V8; H8; Tc8
30	V9
31	V9; H9; Tc9
32	V10
33	V11
34	V12
35–36	V13; H13

37	V14; Tc14
38	V15
39	V16
40–41	V17
42	V18
43	V19
44–50	V20
51–52	H1
53–59 (hyper-)	H2
60–66 (hypo-)	H2
67–68	H3
69	H4
70	H5
71	H6
72–74	H7
75	H8
76–77	H9
78	H10
79	H11
80	H12
81	H14
82–83	H15
84	H16

85–86	H17		135	S5
87	H18		136	S6
88–91	H19		137	S7
92	H20		138	S8
93	Tc1		139	S9
94–98 (hyper-)	Tc2		140	S10
99–100 (hyper-)	Tc2; S2		141	S11
101–106 (hypo-)	Tc2		142	S12
107	Tc3		143	S13
108	Tc4		144	S14; T14
109	Tc5		145	S15
110	Tc6		146	S16; S20
111	Tc7		147–148	S17
112	Tc8		149	S18
113	Tc10		150	S19
114–115	Tc11		151	T1
116	Tc12		152–155 (hyper-)	T2
117	Tc13		156–159 (hypo-)	T2
118–119	Tc15		160	T3
120	Tc16; Tc20		161	T4
121–123	Tc17		162	T5
124	Tc18		163	T6; T7
125	Tc19		164	T8
126	S1		165	T9
127–128 (hyper-)	S2		166	T10
129–132 (hypo-)	S2		167	T11
133	S3		168	T12
134	S4		169	T13

170	T15		207	P20
171	T16; T20		208	Vs1
172–173	T17		209–212 (hyper-)	Vs2
174	T18		213–214 (hypo-)	Vs2
175	T19		215	Vs3
176	P1		216	Vs4
177–179 (hyper-)	P2		217	Vs5
180–183 (hypo-)	P2		218	Vs6
184 (hypo-)	P2; Vs2		219	Vs7
185–186 (hypo-)	P2		220	Vs8
187 (hypo-)	P2; Vs2		221	Vs9
188	P3; Vs3		222	Vs9; Vs13
189	P4		223	Vs10
190–191	P5		224	Vs11
192	P6		225	Vs12
193	P7		226–227	Vs13
194	P8		228	Vs14
195	P9		229	Vs15
196	P10		230	Vs17
197	P11		231	Vs18; Vs20
198	P12		232	Vs19
199	P13			
200–201	P14			
202	P15			
203	P16; Vs16; Vs20			
204	P17			
205	P18			
206	P19			

Appendix 3

Photocopiable Rainbow and Table

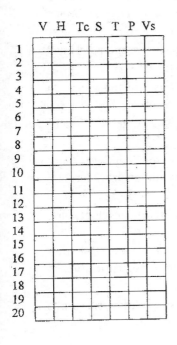

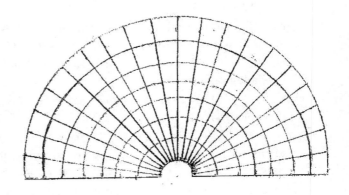

References

Aftanas, E. D. and Zubeck, J. P. (1964) 'Interlimb transfer of changes in tactual activity following occlusion of circumscribed area of the skin.' *Perceptual Motor Skills 18*, 437–442.

Ayres, A. J. (1964) 'Tactile functions: their relation to hyperactive and perceptual motor behavior.' *American Journal of Occupational Therapy 18*, 6–11.

Ayres, A. J. (1979) *Sensory Integration and the Child.* Los Angeles: Western Psychological Services.

Ayres, A. J. (1989) *Sensory Integration and Praxis Tests.* Los Angeles: Western Psychological Services.

Ayres, A. J. and Tickle, L. S. (1980) 'Hyper-responsivity to touch and vestibular stimuli as a predictor of positive response to sensory integration procedures by autistic children.' *American Journal of Occupational Therapy 34*, 375–381.

Baron-Cohen, S. (1996) 'Is there a normal phase of synaesthesia in development?' *PSYCHE 2*, 27, June. http://psyche.cs.monash.edu.au

Baron-Cohen, S., Harrison, J., Goldstein, L. and Wyke, M. (1993) 'Coloured speech perception: Is synaesthesia what happens when modularity breaks down?' *Perception 22*, 419–426.

Baron-Cohen, S., Leslie, A. M. and Frith, U. (1985) 'Does the child with autism have a theory of mind: a case specific developmental delay?' *Cognition 21*, 37–46.

Bauman, M. (1991) 'Microscopic neuroanatomic abnormalities in autism.' *Pediatrics 87*, 791–796.

Berard, G. (1993) *Hearing Equals Behaviour.* New Canaan, CT: Keats.

Berk, R. A. and DeGangi, G. A. (1983) *DeGangi-Berk Test of Sensory Integration.* Los Angeles: Western Psychological Services.

Bill (1997) 'Face Blind: Bill's face blindness (prosopagnosia) pages.' www.choisser.com/faceblind

Blackburn, J. (1997) 'Autism? What is it?' www.autistics.org/library/whatis.html

Blackburn, J. (1999) 'My inside view of autism.' www.planetc.com/urers/ blackjar/autism (site no longer active)

Blackman, L. (2001) *Lucy's Story: Autism and Other Adventures.* London: Jessica Kingsley Publishers.

Blakemore-Brown, L. (2001) *Reweaving the Autistic Tapestry.* London: Jessica Kingsley Publishers.

Blamires, M. (1999) 'Dazzled by the Spectrum: Where should we be looking.' *Autism99 Internet Conference Papers.* www.autism99.org

Bogdashina, O. (2001) 'Possible visual experiences in autism.' www.autismtoday.com/article_possiblevisual

Bovee, J. P. (undated) 'My experiences with autism and how it relates to Theory of Mind.' *Geneva Centre for Autism Publication.* www.autism.net/infoparent

Carter, R. (1998) *Mapping the Mind.* London: Weidenfeld and Nicolson.

Cass, H. (1996) 'Visual impairments and autism – What we know about causation and early identification.' Autism and Visual Impairment Conference. *Sensory Series 5*, 2–24.

Cermak, S. A. (1991) 'Somatodyspraxia.' In A. Fisher, E. Murray and A. Bundy (eds) *Sensory Integration Theory and Practice.* Philadelphia: F. A. Davis.

Cermak, S. and Henderson, A. (1999) 'The efficacy of sensory integration procedures.' www.sinetwork.org

Cesaroni, L. and Garber, M. (1991) 'Exploring the experiences of autism through first-hand accounts.' *Journal of Autism and Developmental Disorders 21*, 3.

Condon, W. S. (1975) 'Multiple response to sound in dysfunctional children.' *Journal of Autism and Childhood Schizophrenia 5*, 37–56.

Cotton, M. M. and Evans, K. M. (1990) 'An evaluation of Irlen lenses as a treatment for specific reading disorders.' *Australian Journal of Psychology 42*, 1, 1–12.

Courchesne, E., Townsend, J., Akshoomoff, N. A., Saitoh, O., Yeung-Courchesne, R., Lincoln, A. J., James, H. E., Haas, R. H., Schreibman, L. and Lau, L. (1994) 'Impairment in shifting attention in autistic and cerebellar patients.' *Behavioral Neuroscience 108*, 848–865.

Cowey, A. and Stoerig, P. (1991) 'The neurology of blindsight.' *Trends in Neuroscience 14*, 140–145.

Cytowic, R. E. (1989) *Synaesthesia: A Union of the Senses.* New York: Springer Verlag.

Cytowic, R. E. (1995) 'Synaesthesia: Phenomenology and neuropsychology. A review of current knowledge.' *PSYCHE 2*, 10. http://psyche.cs.monash.edu.au

Damasio, A. R. and Damasio, H. (1994) 'Cortical systems for retrieval of concrete knowledge: The convergence zone framework.' In C. Koch and J. L. Davis (eds) *Large-scale Neuronal Theories of the Brain.* Cambridge, MA: MIT Press.

Davies, D. R. (1983) 'Attention, arousal and effort.' In A. Gale and J. A. Edwards (eds) *Physiological Correlates of Human Behaviour.* London: Academic Press.

Davis, R. D. (1997) *The Gift of Dyslexia: Why Some of the Smartest People Can't Read and How They Can Learn.* Revised edition. New York: Perigee Books.

Dehay, C., Bullier, J. and Kennedy, H. (1984) 'Transient projections from the fronto-parietal and temporal cortex to areas 17, 18, and 19 in kitten.' *Experimental Brain Research 57*, 208–212.

Dekker, M. (undated) 'On our terms: Emerging autistic culture.' *Autism 99 Internet Conference Papers.* www.autism99.org

Delacato, C. (1974) *The Ultimate Stranger: The Autistic Child.* Noveto, CA: Academic Therapy Publications.

Doman, R. Jr. (1984) 'Sensory Deprivation.' *Journal of the National Academy of Child Development 4.*

Donnelly, J. (1999) 'Speaking for themselves: The thoughts and words of individuals with autism.' *Autism99 Internet Conference Papers.* www.autism99.org

Douglas, V. I. and Peters, K. G. (1979) 'Towards a clearer definition of attention deficit of hyperactive children.' In G. A. Hale and M. Lewis (eds) *Attention and Cognitive Development.* New York: Plenum Press.

Down, J. L. (1887) *On Some of the Mental Affections of Childhood and Youth.* London: Churchill.

Edelson, S. M. and Rimland, B. (2001) *The Efficacy of Auditory Integration Training: Summaries and Critiques of 28 Reports (January, 1993 – May, 2001).* California: Autism Research Institute Publication.

Ellwood, J. (undated) 'Planning aromatherapy activities with your child.' www.aromacaring.co.uk

Farah, M. J. (1989) 'The neural basis of mental imagery.' *Trends in Neuroscience 12*, 395–399.

Farah, M. J. and Feinberg, T. E. (1997) 'Perception and awareness.' In T. E. Feinberg and M. J. Farah (eds) *Behavioral Neurology and Neuropsychology.* New York: McGraw-Hill.

Fay, W. and Schuler, A. (1980) *Emerging Language in Children with Autism*. Baltimore MD: University Park Press.

Feigenberg, I. M. (1986) *To See – to Predict – to Act*. Moscow: Znanie. (In Russian.)

Fisher, A. and Dunn, W. (1983) 'Tactile defensiveness: Historical perspectives, new research – a theory grows.' *Sensory Integration Special Interest Section Newsletter 6*, 2, 3–4.

Fisher, A. and Murray, E. (1991) 'Introduction to sensory integration theory.' In A. Fisher, E. Murray and A. Bundy (eds) *Sensory Integration Theory and Practice*. Philadephia: F.A. Davis Company.

Fleisher, M. (2001) 'Autism: An insider view.' In J. Richer and S. Coates (eds) *Autism: The Search for Coherence*. London: Jessica Kingsley Publishers.

Freeman, B. J. (1993) *Diagnosis of the Syndrome of Autism: Questions Parents Ask*. California: University of California Press.

Frith, U. (1989) *Autism: Explaining the Enigma*. Oxford: Basil Blackwell.

Gainotti, G., Silveri, M. C., Daniele, A. and Giustolisi, L. (1995) 'Neuroanatomical correlates of category-specific semantic disorders: A critical survey.' *Memory 3*, 247–264.

Garner, I. and Hamilton, D. (2001) 'Evidence for central coherence: Children with autism do experience visual illusions.' In J. Richer and S. Coates (eds) *Autism: The Search for Coherence*. London: Jessica Kingsley Publishers.

Gazzaniga, M. S. (1988) 'Brain modularity: Towards a philosophy of conscious experience.' In A. J. Marcel and E. Bisiach (eds) *Consciousness in Contemporary Science*. Oxford: Clarendon Press.

Gense, M. H. and Gense, D. J. (1994) 'Identifying autism in children with blindness and visual impairment.' *Review 26*, 56–62.

Gerland, G. (1997) *A Real Person – Life on the Outside*. London: Souvenir Press.

Gerland, G. (1998) 'Now is the time! Autism and psychoanalysis.' *Code of Good Practice on Prevention of Violence against Persons with Autism*. The DAPHNE Initiative of the European Commission: Autism-Europe publication.

Gibson, E. J. (1969) *Principles of Perceptual Learning and Perceptual Development*. New York: Appleton Century Croft.

Gillingham, G. (1991) 'Autism: Disability or superability.' *Collected Papers: Therapeutic Approaches to Autism. Research and Practice*. Sunderland: University of Sunderland Enterprises Ltd.

Grandin, T. (1996a) *Thinking in Pictures and Other Reports from My Life with Autism*. New York: Vintage Books.

Grandin, T. (1996b) 'My experiences with visual thinking, sensory problems and communication difficulties.' Centre for the Study of Autism. www.autism.org/temple/visual.html

Grandin, T. (1999) 'Genius may be an abnormality: Educating students with Asperger's Syndrome or high functioning autism.' *Autism99 Internet Conference Papers.* www.autism99.org

Grandin, T. (2000) 'My mind is a web browser: How people with autism think.' *Cerebrum 2*, 1 Winter, 14–22.

Grandin, T. and Scariano, M. (1986) *Emergence: Labeled Autistic.* Novato, CA: Arena Press.

Happe, F. (1994) *Autism: An Introduction to Psychological Theory.* London: UCL Press.

Happe, F. (1996) 'Studying weak central coherence at low levels: Children with autism do not succumb to visual illusions. A research note.' *Journal of Child Psychology and Psychiatry 37*, 873–877.

Happe, F. (1999) 'Why success is more interesting than failure: Understanding assets and deficits in autism.' *Autism Conference Papers*, Oxford, 17-19 Sept. (Unpublished).

Hatch-Rasmussen, C. (1995) 'Sensory Integration.' www.autism.org

Herron, E. (1993) *Sensory Integration.* Fact Sheet, No 8. www.smsu.edu/Access/fact8.html

Hutt, S. J., Hutt, C., Lee, D. and Ounsted, C. (1964) 'Arousal and childhood autism.' *Nature 204*, 908–909.

Irlen, H. (1989) 'Improving reading problems due to symptoms of Scotopic Sensitivity Syndrome using Irlen lenses and overlays.' *Education 109*, 413–417.

Irlen, H. (1991) *Reading by the Colors: Overcoming Dyslexia and other Reading Disabilities through the Irlen Method.* New York: Avery.

Irlen, H. (1997) 'Reading problems and Irlen coloured lenses.' *Dyslexia Review 8*, 5, 4–7.

Jackson, L. (2002) *Freaks, Geeks and Asperger Syndrome: A User Guide to Adolescence.* London: Jessica Kingsley Publishers.

Joan and Rich (1999) *What is Autism?* www.ani.autistics.org/joanrich.html

Joliffe, T. and Baron-Cohen, S. (1997) 'Are people with autism and Asperger Syndrome faster than normal on the embedded figures test?' *Journal of Child Psychology and Psychiatry 38*, 5, 527–534.

Joliffe, T., Lakesdown, R. and Robinson, C. (1992) 'Autism, a personal account.' *Communication 26*, 3, 12–19.

Jordan, D. (1972) *Dyslexia in the Classroom.* Columbus Ohio: Merrill.

Jordan, R. and Powell, S. (1990) *The Special Curricular Needs of Autistic Children: Learning and Thinking Skills.* London: The Association of Heads and Teachers of Adults and Children with Autism.

Jordan, R. and Powell, S. (1995) *Understanding and Teaching Children with Autism.* Chichester: John Wiley and Sons.

Kanner, L. (1943) 'Autistic disturbances of affective contact.' *Nervous Child 2,* 217–250.

Kanner, L. (1946) 'Irrelevant and metaphorical language in early infantile autism.' *American Journal of Psychiatry 103,* 242–246.

Kanner, L. (1971) 'Follow-up study of eleven autistic children, originally reported in 1943.' *Journal of Autism and Childhood Schizophrenia 2,* 119–145.

Kapes, B. (2001) 'Sensory integration disorder.' *Gale Encyclopedia of Alternative Medicine.* Gale Group. www.findarticles.com

King, L. J. (1989) 'Facilitating neurodevelopment: The bridge between therapy and education.' *The National Conference of the Autistic Society Papers.* www.cirs.org/homepage/cns/fn.htm

Knickerbocker, B. (1980) *A Holistic Approach to Learning Disabilities.* Thorofare, NJ: Charles B. Slack.

Kochmeister, S. (1995) 'Excerpts from "Shattering Walls".' *Facilitated Communication Digest 5,* 3, 9–11.

Koegel, R. L. and Schreibman, L. (1976) 'Identification of consistent responding to auditory stimuli by functionally "deaf" autistic child.' *Journal of Autism and Childhood Schizophrenia 6,* 147–156.

Koomar, J. and Bundy, A. (1991) 'The art and science of creating direct intervention from theory.' In A. Fisher, E. Murray and A. Bundy (eds) *Sensory Integration Theory and Practice.* Philadelphia: F. A. Davis.

Kracke, I. (1994) 'Developmental prosopagnosia in Asperger syndrome: Presentation and discussion of an individual case.' *Developmental Medicine and Child Neurology 36,* 873–886.

Kraemer, G. (1985) 'Effects of differences in early social experience on primate neurobiological-behavioural development.' In M. Reite and T. Field (eds) *The Psychobiology of Attachment and Separation.* New York: Academic Press.

Kranowitz, C. (1998) *The Out of Sync Child: Recognizing and Coping with Sensory Integration.* New York: The Berkley Publishing Group.

Lane, D. M. and Pearson, D. A. (1982) 'The development of selective attention.' *Merrill-Palmer Quarterly 28,* 317–337.

Lawson, W. (1998) *Life Behind Glass: A Personal Account of Autism Spectrum Disorder.* Lismore, Australia: Southern Cross University Press.

Lawson, W. (1999) 'Reflection on autism and communication: A personal account.' *Autism99 Internet Conference Papers.* www.autism99.org

Lawson, W. (2001) *Understanding and Working with the Spectrum of Autism: An Insider's View.* London: Jessica Kingsley Publishers.

Legge, B. (2002) *Can't Eat, Won't Eat.* London: Jessica Kingsley Publishers.

Lemley, B. (1999) 'Do you see what they see?' *Discover 20*, 12.

Longhorn, F. (1993) *Planning a Multi-sensory Massage Programme for Very Special People.* London: Catalyst Education Resources Limited.

Lovaas, O. I., Schreibman, L., Koegel, R. L. and Rehm, R. (1971) 'Selective responding by autistic children to multiple sensory input.' *Journal of Abnormal Psychology 77*, 211–222.

Luria, A. R. (1987) *The Mind of a Mnemonist.* Cambridge, MA: Harvard University Press.

McKean, T. (1994) *Soon Will Come the Light.* Arlington, TX: Future Education.

Maurer, D. (1993) 'Neonatal synaesthesia: implications for the processing of speech and faces.' In B. de Boysson-Bardies, S. de Schonen, P. Jusczyk, P. McNeilage and J. Morton (eds) *Developmental Neurocognition: Speech and Face Processing in the First Year of Life.* Dordrecht: Kluwer Academic Publishers.

Meares, O. (1980) 'Figure/ground, brightness contrast and reading disabilities.' *Visible Language XIV*, 1, 13–29.

Melzack, R. and Burns, S. K. (1965) 'Neurophysiological effects of early sensory restriction.' *Experimental Neurology 13*, 163–175.

Morris, B. (1999) 'New light and insight, on an old matter.' *Autism99 Internet Conference Papers.* www.autism99.org

Mukhopadhyay, R. (Tito) (1999) 'When silence speaks: The way my mother taught me.' *Autism99 Internet Conference Papers.* www.autism99.org

Murray, D. K. C. (1992) 'Attention tunnelling and autism.' In P. Shattock and G. Linfoot (eds) *Living with Autism: The Individual, the Family, and the Professional.* Sunderland: Autism Research Unit, University of Sunderland.

Myles, B. S., Cook, K. T., Miller, N. E., Rinner, L. and Robbins, L. A. (2001) *Asperger Syndrome and Sensory Issues.* Shawnee Mission Knsas: Autism Asperger Publishing Co.

Nelson, S. (undated) 'Sensory Integration Dysfunction: The Misunderstood, Misdiagnosed and Unseen Disability.' www.hunnybee.com.au/autism/sensoryintegration.

Nony (1993) 'Speculation on light sensitivity.' *Our Voice 3*, 1.

O'Neill, J. L. (1999) *Through the Eyes of Aliens: A Book about Autistic People.* London: Jessica Kingsley Publishers.

O'Neill, J. L. (2000) *I Live in a Home within Myself.* The NAS publication. http://w02-0211.web.dircon.net/peoplew/personal/jasmine.html

Ornitz, E. M. (1969) 'Disorders of perception common to early infantile autism and schizophrenia.' *Comprehensive Psychiatry 10*, 259–274.

Ornitz, E. M. (1974) 'The modulation of sensory input and motor output in autistic children.' *Journal of Autism and Childhood Schizophrenia 4*, 197–215.

Ornitz, E. M. (1983) 'The functional neuroanatomy of infantile autism.' *International Journal of Neuroscience 19*, 85–124.

Ornitz, E. M. (1985) 'Neurophysiology of infantile autism.' *Journal of the American Academy of Child Psychiatry 24*, 251–262.

Ornitz, E. M. (1989) 'Autism at the interface between sensory and information processing.' In G. Dawson (ed) *Autism: Nature, Diagnosis and Treatment.* New York: Guilford.

Ornitz, E. M., Guthrie, D. and Farley, A. J. (1977) 'The early development of autistic children.' *Journal of Autism and Childhood Schizophrenia 7*, 207–229.

Ornitz, E. M., Guthrie, D. and Farley, A. J. (1978) 'The early symptoms of childhood autism.' In G. Serban (ed) *Cognitive Deficits in the Development of Mental Illness.* New York: Brunner/Mazel.

Ornitz, E. M. and Ritvo, E. R. (1968) 'Perceptual inconsistency in early infantile autism.' *Archives of General Psychiatry 18*, 76–98.

Orton, S. T. (1928) 'Specific reading disability – strephosymbolia.' *Journal of the American Medical Association 90*, 1095–1099.

Ozonoff, S. (1995) 'Executive function in autism.' In E. Schopler and G. B. Mesibov (eds) *Diagnosis and Assessment in Autism.* New York: Plenum Press.

Ozonoff, S., Roger, S. J. C. and Pennington, B. F. (1991) 'Asperger's syndrome: Evidence of empirical distinction from high functioning autism.' *Journal of Child Psychology and Psychiatry 32*, 1107–1122.

Ozonoff, S., Strayer, D. L., McMahon, W. M. and Filloux, F. (1994) 'Executive function abilities in autism and Tourette syndrome: An information processing approach.' *Journal of Child Psychology and Psychiatry 35*, 6, 1015–1032.

Parham, L. D. and Mailloux, Z. (1996) 'Sensory integration.' In J. Case-Smith, A. S. Allen and P. N. Pratt (eds) *Occupational Therapy for Children* (3rd edn). St. Louis, MO: Mosby.

Park, C. C. (1967) *The Siege: The First Eight Years of an Autistic Child.* Boston, MA: Little, Brown.

Park, D. C. and Yourderian, P. (1974) 'Light and number: Ordering principles in the world of an autistic child.' *Journal of Autism and Childhood Schizophrenia 4,* 313–323.

Pemberton, A (1999). 'Irlen Scotopic Sensitivity: The link to autism.' *Autism99 Internet Conference Papers.* www.autism99.org

Posner, M. (1975) 'Psychobiology of attention.' In M. S. Gazzaniga and C. Blakemore (eds) *Handbook of Psychobiology.* New York: Academy Press.

Powell, S. (2000) 'Learning about life asocially: The autistic perspective on education.' In S. Powell (ed) *Helping Children with Autism to Learn.* London: David Fulton Publishers.

Rand, B. (undated) 'How to understand people who are different.' www.hunnybee.com/autism/bradrand.html

Ratey, J. (2001) *A User's Guide to the Brain.* London: Little, Brown and Company.

Riley, D. (1999) *Understanding Irlen Syndrome.* Www.irelen.org.uk/Homepage.htm

Rimland, B. (1964) *Infantile Autism: The Syndrome and Its Implications for a Neural Therapy of Behavior.* New York: Appleton Century Crofts.

Rimland, B. (1978) 'Inside the mind of the autistic savant.' *Psychology Today,* August 1978.

Robinson, G. L. (1996) 'Irlen lenses and adults: Preliminary results of a controlled study of reading speed, accuracy and comprehension.' *The 4th International Irelen Conference Papers,* 27–28 September, Sydney. California: Irlen Institute Press.

Robinson, G. L. (1998) 'Another possible causal variable for symptoms of SS/IS? Preliminary results for a pilot study of biochemical anomalies.' *The 5th International Irlen Conference Papers,* 1–3 July, Cambridge, UK. California: Irlen Institute Press.

Rose, S. (1993) *The Making of Memory: From Molecules to Mind.* London: Bantam Press.

Royeen, C. (1989) 'Commentary of "Tactile functions in learning disabled and normal children: Reliability and validity considerations".' *Occupational Therapy Journal of Research 9,* 16–23.

Russell, J. (1994) 'Agency and early mental development.' In J. Bermudez, A. J. Marcel and N. Eilan (eds) *The Body and the Self.* Cambridge MA: MIT Press.

Sacks, O. (1995) *An Anthropologist on Mars.* London: Picador.

Sainsbury, C. (2000) 'Holding therapy: An autistic perspective.' www.nas.org.uk/pubs/archive/hold.html

Schatzman, M. (1980) *The Story of Ruth.* London: Gerald Duckworth.

Shah, A. and Frith, U. (1993) 'Why do autistic individuals show superior performance on the block design task?' *Journal of Child Psychology and Psychiatry 34*, 8, 1351–1364.

Sheldrake, R. (1999) *Dogs That Know When Their Owners Are Coming Home.* California: Hutchinson.

Siegel, B. (1996) *The World of the Autistic Child.* New York: Oxford University Press.

Simon, D. and Land, P. (1987) 'Early tactile stimulation influences organization of somatic sensory cortex.' *Nature 326*, 694–697.

Sinclair, J. (1992) 'Bridging the gaps: An inside view of autism.' In E. Schopler and G. B. Mesibov (eds) *High-functioning Individuals with Autism.* New York: Plenum Press.

Sinclair, J. (1993) 'Don't mourn for us.' *Our Voice 1*, 3.

Sinclair, J. (1998) 'Is cure a goal?' www.members.xoom.com/JimSinclair

Snyder, A. W. and Mitchell, J. D. (1999) 'Is integer arithmetic fundamental to mental proceeding? The mind's secret arithmetic.' *Proceedings of the Royal Society of London 266*, 587–592.

Sperber, D. and Wilson, D. (1986) *Relevance: Communication and Cognition.* Oxford: Blackwell.

Stehli, A. (1991) *Sound of a Miracle: A Child's Triumph Over Autism.* New York: Avon Books.

Stephens, L. C. (1997) 'Sensory integration dysfunction in young children.' *AAHBEI News Exchange 2*, 1.

Tomatis, A. A. (1991) *The Conscious Ear.* New York: Station Hill Press.

Tustin, F. (1974) *Autism and Childhood Psychosis.* London: Hogarth Press.

VanDalen, J. G. T. (1995) 'Autism from within: Looking through the eyes of a mildly afflicted autistic person.' *Link 17*, 11–16.

Volkmar, F. R., Cohen, D. J. and Paul, R. (1986) 'An evaluation of DSM-III criteria for infantile autism.' *Journal of American Academy of Child Psychiatry 25*, 190–197.

Walker, N. and Cantello, J. (eds) (1994) 'You don't have words to describe what I experience.' www.autism.net/infoparent.html

Waterhouse, S. (2000) *A Positive Approach to Autism.* London: Jessica Kingsley Publishers.

Weiskrantz, L. (1986) *Blindsight: A Case Study and Implications.* Oxford: Oxford University Press.

White, B. B. and White, M. S. (1987) 'Autism from inside.' *Medical Hypotheses 24.*

Wilbarger, P. (1995) 'The sensory diet: Activity programs based on sensory processing theory.' *Sensory Integration Special Interest Section Newsletter 18,* 1–4.

Wilbarger, J. L. and Stackhouse, T. M. (1998) 'Sensory modulation: A review of the literature.' www.ot-innovations.com/sensory_modulation

Wilbarger, P. and Wilbarger, J. L. (1991) *Sensory Defensiveness in Children Aged 2–12: An Intervention Guide for Parents and Other Caretakers.* Santa Barbara, CA: Avanti Educational Programs.

Wilkins, A. (1995) *Visual Stress.* Oxford: Oxford Science Publications.

Willey, L. H. (1999) *Pretending to Be Normal.* London: Jessica Kingsley Publishers.

Williams, D. (1992) *Nobody Nowhere.* London: Doubleday.

Williams, D. (1994) *Somebody Somewhere.* London: Doubleday.

Williams, D. (1996) *Autism. An Inside-Out Approach.* London: Jessica Kingsley Publishers.

Williams, D. (1998) *Autism and Sensing. The Unlost Instinct.* London: Jessica Kingsley Publishers.

Williams, D. (1999) *Like Colour to the Blind: Soul Searching and Soul Finding.* London: Jessica Kingsley Publishers.

Wing, L. (1992) *The Triad of Impairments of Social Interaction: An Aid to Diagnosis.* London: NAS.

Winter, S. (1987) 'Irlen lenses: An appraisal.' *Australian Educational and Developmental Psychologist 5,* 7–10.

Zeki, S. (1992) 'The visual image in the mind and brain.' *Scientific American 267,* 3, 42–50.

Subject Index

'accumulation of unknown knowing' 79, 83, 91
Applied Behaviour Analysis 62, 181
aromatherapy 159
attention 40, 51, 67, 100, 105
  in autism 100–5
  delay in switching 103
  directed 101
  idiosyncratic focus 102
  joint 103–4
  selective 101
  tunnelling 102 (*see also* monotropism)
Attention Deficit Hyperactivity Disorder 103, 141, 144
auditory impairments 25, 143 (*see also* deafness)
Auditory Integration Treatment (AIT) 144
autism 19–20
  as a way of being 20
  as sensory dysfunction 25
  diagnosis 20
  misunderstanding 22, 28
  theories of 21 (*see also* theory of mind)
autistic savant 45, 48, 103, 105, 107 (*see also* Nadia; Wiltshire, Stephen)
  attentional mechanism of 103
  skills 100
avoidance of direct perception 83, 86, 88, 179 (*see also* peripheral perception)

behavioural optometry 151
Berard method 146–8
blind spot 32

blindness 27, 38, 92, 143, 171 (*see also* visual impairments)

central auditory processing disorder 119, 128, 142
central coherence 21, 47, 84, 102
  monotropic central coherence 84
  weak central coherence, theory of 21, 47, 51, 68, 69, 102
cognitive style 52, 98
concept 37
  formation 98, 109
  tactile-motor 38

daydreaming 22, 83, 95–6, 165
deafness 26, 38–9, 143, 171 (*see also* auditory impairments)
delayed processing 49, 52, 76–9, 92, 103, 108, 160, 163, 178
desensitization 154, 156
'distance touching' 88
distorted perception 28, 38, 52, 73–4, 79, 92, 163
disturbance by stimuli 52, 61–5, 162, 176
disturbances of sensory modulation 66, 137, 139, 142 (*see also* sensory modulation disorder)

executive function deficit 116–7
eye contact 87, 156, 179
  avoidance 86, 88, 164

face-blindness 127–8 (*see also* prosopagnosia)
fascination with stimuli 52, 61, 64–5, 93, 162, 177

Author Index